Luxury Watches
A Purchasing Guide

Leonard Lowe

2016-11-03

Testimonials

4/5 Stars **** Good reference for those considering a luxury watch: »Good overview of luxury watch manufacturers and significance of each. Reviews some leading models. Covers reasons to invest in a luxury watch. Easily readable.« JJPEngr

4/5 Stars **** »The information contained in this book is quite useful« Juan C. L

4/5 Stars **** »Four Stars. Involving.« Aaron

»I enjoyed the book and now must rob a bank to afford a Rolex or Patek-Philippe.« John G.

»That was an interesting book. I am ready to move up to luxury.« John F.

And don't forget to share this ebook with your friends at. . .
Facebook - Twitter - Pinterest - Tumblr - Reddit

The Book

A luxury watch is more than $5,000. So naturally in this topic there is a lot of money involved. This book will help you to avoid wrong decisions that would cost you huge amounts of money. It will help you to understand how the luxury watch market works. There are a lot of watchmakers and even more watches on the market. It will help you to identify the top brands and watches that not only look nice, but are a good investment into the future. Vintages models are very en vogue for some years now. So if you consider purchasing a luxury watch, there are a lot of things you need to know. Like e.g. What is a luxury watch and what makes it so expensive? What models and brands keep their value over years, which even grow in value? What are the top watch brands of the world? What are the top watch models, the timeless classics available? Should I buy a replica watch? Can a luxury watch be a financial investment like artworks, oldtimers or precious metals? This book will help you with basic knowledge and some personal advice.

The Author

Leonard Lowe is a german engineer, scientific researcher and professor for mechanical engineering. Throughout his career his success formula was always 'never believe, always question – never stand still, always learn – never accept, always understand'.

He is the author of several books on technology, nature, philosophy, history and politics.

Beyond his professional live he is a tech and hi-tech enthusiast, computer geek, brillant thinker and writer. He loves to acquire knowledge and share it. His sharp analyses and unusual views help his readers making the right decisions in many different areas of life.

Online Book Stores

Books from THINK-eBooks are available at

http://think-ebooks.com/where-to-buy/

We thank Rolex S.A., Patek Philippe S.A., Audemars Piguet S.A., Breitling S.A., Panerai S.A., Omega S.A., Hublot S.A. IWC S.A., Jaeger-LeCoultre S.A., Eterna S.A., and A. Lange AG for their kind support.

Imprint

ISBN: 978-3-7393-2911-6

Contents

Part 1

The Basics

1.1 What is a Luxury Watch?

It's not so obvious at all. There are a lot of watchmakers all over the world that make great looking watches for men and women. And a lot of them charge huge amounts of money for their watches. There are hundreds of brands, manufacturers, makers, all over the place. And they all intend to participate in that great market full of luxury money.

But is it that, what defines a luxury watch? A high, a sometimes unbelievable high pricetag? We are talking about e.g. $180,000 for a Richard Mille. But don't think that there is nobody on the planet who would purchase a wristwatch for that kind of money. Richard Mille finds about 3000 people every year who buy their products.

No, it is not only the price. Charging extreme money for something does not make the maker a top brand and the product a real luxury product. It is not about what they pretend, but what you assume.

Indeed only a few of these makers of expensive watches do really have an outstanding reputation as a luxury watchmaker. Others haven't and are equally expensive or even more expensive.

This reputation, to be honest, is not entirely based on facts like e.g. a superior accuracy, outstanding robustness or fancy functionality – not even on the use of luxury materials like gold or platinum. The awful truth is: reputation always is and ever was a mixture of factors like heritage and image of the brand, scarcity of its models and other rather subjective factors.

To make things even more obscure, *every* relevant luxury watch-maker is – has to be – from Switzerland. Only a Swiss watch is a real luxury watch. The Swiss watch industry managed to establish kind of a monopolistic position. There are very few exceptions with a equally high reputation, like A. Lange from Germany. But that is just an exception to the rule.

1.2   What is an automatic watch?

A quartz-watch is not a luxury watch. If you consider to purchase a luxury watch, forget quartz.

Yes, a quartz watch is the most accurate kind of watch, you never have to wind it, it only needs a new battery every half a dozen years and it can be as tiny as a fingernail as the quartz movement does not need a lot of space because all the functionality of the watch is packed into a tiny computer chip. And when you combine that technology with radio, you can have atomic precision and always the correct daylight savings time. But if you are talking 'real watches', that is technology-nonsense.

All that modern technology has nothing to do with expensive luxury watches. If you want a watch to find out what time it is, grab a Seiko quartz watch for a few bucks and be happy with it.

The same applies for smart watches. If you want to carry a computer on your wrist, do so. But despite its price it will never be a luxury watch. I am a huge Apple-Fan, but I will never consider an Apple Watch as a luxury watch. It's a gadget, it's a cool little computer, very close to you, it's a lot of things, but it will never be a luxury watch, even if they price it at $50,000.

And that is because it is not timeless. It sounds like joke, but only timeless watches are real luxury watches. If you take a Rolex watch from 1930 or a Omega pocket watch from 1910, it still works, when you wind it. It works as it did in 1930 or 1910. And it will continue to work long after we passed away, just like its former owners already have passed away. If you purchase a luxury watch it keeps its value, because it keeps working. It does not depend on the availability of batteries, or even voltage, it does not need an atomic clock somewhere to synchronize to, nothing. It just works completely by itself – and of course you, setting the right time, once.

That means also: a real watch needs to be a mechanical watch. If you need a battery to have it working, it's not timeless. A mechanical watch is a piece of art and engineering. It is a living thing, it ticks like your heart beats, only 28,800 times every hour – your heart does a mere 6,000 beats during that time. The watch never stands still, like your heart. It's a piece of art, technology, a living thing – not a boring, battery driven computer chip.

And it might become even more. Think about it: what is left from a person long gone? Often it is his watch – and not much more than that. You may have watches from the early 20th century, even dating back to the 19th century. It is a most personal thing of a person, a relative, a grand-grand-grand-uncle, someone, you have no other record of, other than this watch. It is a piece to remember your ancestors and remember your own mortality. I tells you to try now, because tomorrow may already be too late – whatever it may be you want to accomplish.

So a good watch is a timeless piece, because it is a mechanical watch. And often it is even more, it may be a way to live on in the memory of your children, grandchildren and even grandgrand-children for being the guy with the old watch. It sometimes may be the only way to stay a little bit longer in their memory.

So you need a timeless mechanical watch that will be handed down in your family and will remind later generations that you were there. And what mechanical watch? Aren't there lots of different types?

No, it's quite simple. Mechanical watches come in exactly two flavors:

1. manual wind

2. automatic

And that's it.

The difference is simple: the automatic watch movement has a self winding mechanism that uses every little move you make with the watch on your wrist to wind the watch. It is the first and oldest form of energy harvesting known to mankind. And the first watchmaker that built watches for a larger market with that technology was Rolex.

Summing up: the basic rule is quite simple: if you want a real luxury watch, you have to purchase a mechanical watch with either an manual wind or an automatic wind movement. And it has to be made in Switzerland. Luxury has nothing to do with electronics, it has nothing to do with diamonds placed on its case, it does not even need to be made from gold. It's all about timelessness in style and its whole being – that's the secret.

1.3   Where to buy a luxury watch?

The watch market has some peculiarities. When you go to your local watch dealer, you will find either of these scenarios:

1. he does not offer any of the top brands as these sell their watches only by selected distributors, so called 'Konzessionäre'

2. he offers the brands, but most of the watches (esp. the interesting sports models) are out of stock and will only be available within months or even years

That is because the watchmakers found out a simple psychological rule of selling: if you sell less than you actually can, demand will increase dramatically. What you must understand is that people from Switzerland are extremely good in making money. They are famous for that ability.

What they do is a two-step process. First step is: if a watch dealer orders 5 pieces of an expensive watch, deliver 2. The 3 watches you could have also sold, is an investment into the future. It reduces your turnover today, but the strategy will pay off later. The second step is: increase the price for the 2 watches you ship dramatically over time. At least 10% every year. The result is that a customer has to wait for a watch like e.g. the Rolex Daytona steel for up to 10 years. It becomes real luxury just to have one.

The watch dealer market is divided into two sectors: one, the official dealers, that have the concession of the watchmakers to sell their watches, but often do not have the really interesting watch models in stock. Two, the so called grey market, that have some of the interesting models sometimes even for a good price. The latter are dealers that sell watches unofficially. That is not illegal, as you can purchase and sell luxury watches like any other product, but they do this without the official concession of the watchmakers. And that is a real drawback for the buyer.

If you intend to purchase a luxury watch I strongly recommend to purchase it from an official dealer. Here comes why:

Take Rolex as an example. A Rolex watch is not just expensive, because Rolex fancies a rather ridiculous pricing policy – even if most people think of it like that. A Rolex also is expensive because Rolex does a lot of research and development on every part of the watch – and R&D, as we all know, costs loads of money. They develop not only their casings and movements completely by themselves, they develop their own steel that is shiny and rugged at the same time, they cast their own parts, they hold several patents to make the watch waterproof and robust. All that seems to be low tech, but if you aim to perfection everything becomes hard to do.

But there are other ›Rolex‹ watches on the market as well. Watches that are manufactured without all that jazz. These are fake Rolex watches, so called ›replicas‹ or ›homages‹. Don't be fooled: these are fake watches and are product piracy. Nothing more than that. But these fake watches are not always looking like crab any more these days, like they did some years ago. Today they look almost exactly like the original ones and feature the trademarked Rolex brand names and symbols (what makes them totally illegal). Today you sometimes need to be an expert to distinguish the replica from the real one. And that is a high risk for the buyer in the grey market.

And there is even more risk by something that is called Frankenstein watches. It is basically the combination of parts from several watches to create a very sought after model that sells for an extremely high price. The danger here is that you do not get a fake part, but all original parts, that just do not belong together. The more aggressive criminals even combine original parts (obviously the parts you can see, like the case and the dial) with fake crab parts (the parts you cannot see so easily like the movement) to create a worthless piece they can sell for a very high price.

A replica of a let's say $10,000 Rolex model only costs $300 or $1,000. Some even have mechanical movements. This is of course all highly illegal. The Frankenstein version will even cost you the same $10,000 like the flawless original, but it is partly or even utterly worthless.

But as an amateur you can easily be tricked into purchasing one of those perfect looking replica watches – for the full Rolex price. That would be a major mistake as these are absolutely worthless. They are not even worth their price of $300 or $1,000 you can purchase them for, knowing that they are replica watches, simply because they are illegal! You cannot sell them any more, e.g. on ebay or elsewhere. They're just dead meat. In my opinion there's a real risk of getting sold one of these well made replicas instead of a real Rolex, what basically means, your money is down the drain.

If you purchase from a official Rolex dealer, you can be sure to get a real one. Additionally Rolex does a lot to make sure you got a real one and nowadays tries to keep track of all the watches they sell in a database, so they know where they are. And if you purchase one, you can ask Rolex, if they registered it and if it's a real one. If you purchase a new one, the dealer will transfer its serial number to Rolex, along with the dealer's name, the date when it was purchased and the city, so Rolex knows which watches have been sold roughly where on the planet. And only Rolex knows that information, so nobody is able to misuse it.

A grey market watch dealer cannot do all that. So the risk is completely on the buyers side.

Part 2

The Watchmakers

2.1 What are the Top Watch Brands?

If you purchase a luxury watch, you want a ›real‹ luxury watch,
not just some ridiculously expensive watch. And there are not so
many top shelf luxury watch manufacturers as you might expect.
The top three watchmakers of this world are ironically called the
›holy trinity‹, they are: PP, AP and VC. That is:

1. Patek Phillippe

2. Audemars Piguet

3. Vacheron Constantin

If you'd like to put it like that, this is Rolls Royce, Ferrari and
Aston Martin of the watch industry. These are the holy ones, the
apex, the absolute top – and they are in this position for a very
long time already.

Perhaps you wonder that you never heard these names before.
Perhaps you even wonder where Rolex is on that list. Think of it
that way: »Every watch enthusiast must have at least one watch
from a watchmaker he cannot pronounce the name properly.«

The truth is: compared to these, a Rolex is literally cheap.
The holy trinity members do not sell watches below $20,000 – that

is per piece. And that might be why you never heard of them before, as their customer base is rather narrow. Partly they have that price because these manufacturers do not offer watches that are made from materials other than massive gold, whitegold or platinum.

There is always an exception to every rule: AP shocked the world of watchmaking in the early 1970s with their model ›Royal Oak‹ that was made of stainless steel. A sacrilege, als all luxury watches up to that time had to be made from gold.

And that is why the today highly appreciated Rolex steel sports models from the 1960s had back then not been considered being luxury watches at all. They were just 'tool watches'. They were made for a purpose, like, giving a diver the right time under water. A place where other watches usually ceased working and took major damage due to the sea water. These today considered 'vintage' Rolex models were never conceived to be luxury pieces but are today considered to be. A Rolex Daytona from that era today is sold for about $30,000 to $100,000, even if it could be purchased back then for $200 – and nobody really wanted it. It basically was sold so seldomly that it today is scarce enough to be a real collectors item.

But to be honest, despite its lesser material of steel, even the Royal Oak wasn't much cheaper than the others – and still isn't today.

In the row behind the holy trinity there are watchmakers that do not have exactly the reputation of the three leading brands, but do quite well either. These might be:

1. A. Lange

2. Jaeger-LeCoultre

3. Breguet

A. Lange from Germany is the unexpected exception to the rule. They make absolutely stunningly brilliant watches with only one drawback: they are not from Switzerland. If they were, they would probably considered to be the fourth member of the 'holy trinity'. Some experts even say, A. Lange is better than the holy trinity pieces.

Then there is Jaeger-LeCoultre, who is considered to be the watchmakers watchmaker, as no other watchmaker has done so many movements even for Patek and other top brands as JLC. And JLC watches to this day are avant-garde in design and technology. Jaeger-LeCoultre seems to me the most underrated watchmaker of them all. Their designs are often avant-garde, their technology is focussed on the movements. But they have kind of an image problem that – in my opinion – could be related to their rather complicated brand name. It might be as simple as that, because their products are much better than JLCs market recognition.

Every watchmaker has its history. Some started out as makers of dials, others as makers of nice cases, others even only as resellers. JLC started out as a maker of movements. And over time JLC made movements for a lot of big names. What ETA is today for the Swiss mass market, in some sense JLC was for the high horology sector: the watchmaker of the watchmakers.

Breguet is the traditionalist in this sector. They are in this position for a really long time and their reputation comes mainly from inventions they made in the early 1800s.

Finally there is the heart and soul, the core of the luxury watch segment concerning sales figures and quality and this might be these fellows:

1. Rolex

2. Omega

3. Breitling

4. IWC

5. Hublot

These all sell watches for at least $5,000 and thus they form the core of the luxury watch segment. All these do or at least try to manufacture their own movements, what in essence parts them from the other watchmakers that basically all use standard movements and put these in their nice looking watch cases.

But they are quite different at the core. Rolex is the leading figure in luxury watchmaking and really makes workhorses with a long lifespan. Omega much more than Rolex tends to mass production, market coverage and fancy designs that reflect the trends of the time. Breitling tries more than really is a luxury watchmaker and makes a lot of noise with their pilot chronographs. Breitling at the core seems to be very rugged, very reliable, with a high technological standard. IWC is more a serious military supplier than a luxury watch maker. Only some models with their own inhouse movements can be considered at the standard of Rolex or Breitling. Hublot sinally simply makes millionairs' toys – very cool and very stylish.

The others behind these top brands are legion and you know a lot of them: even some great names from former ages, like Tag Heuer, Longines, Chopard, Piguet, Rado, Eterna, but also mere makers of fashion cases like Baume & Mercier, Jaques Lemans and all the many others.

All of those still use mechanical automatic Swiss made movements in their watches, but they all use the same movements from one single manufacturer called ETA. These movements are not bad either and they are Swiss made too. But the fact that these brands do not make their own movements reduces their reputation to that of a mere designer of nice housings and bracelets instead of a serious watchmaker – as the movement is the core of the watch and the thing that really matters, right? To again use the car analogy and say it in a different form: would you buy a Porsche that uses a Ford engine? Is this the real thing? Even if it still does 200 mph? I think, no, it isn't at all! At least not to an enthusiast, who loves the detail. Most certainly not to the purist who is into cleanness and originality. And of course not for the collector, who gives the watches its long term value. So what's it worth then? Simple: the usage. But not more than that.

And here is another interesting view to look at this market: the luxury watch market is somehow in a very special position. If you think of other luxury products, they are either rip off like clothes or handbags, because very soon they are so utterly worthless, that some handbag-manufacturer in Paris burns all handbags from the last year in a special event. And other luxury products are downright too expensive to be in reach of any average person. A luxury car e.g. is easily more than $100,000 or $250,000 and a luxury house is easily more than $1,000,000.

But a luxury watch is a real luxury product, what means it has a long term value, but at a pricetag that nearly everyone in the first world can afford. It is a luxury product that is also available for the average, or slightly over-average class.

And that makes it such an interesting market. They have the value-storing effect like ›real‹ and no-rip-off luxury products, but in a minimum price range of not more than acceptable $5,000 to $15,000, what makes them affordable for a much broader range of customers. Interesting.

2.2 Are Swiss Watches an Investment?

Switzerland is famous for? Watches, cheese, army knives and... bank accounts. But has this something to do with watches? This might look like a silly question. Of course not, they are just watches, right?

Wrong.

There are wristwatches – and not only a few – that cost more than $50,000, some more than $100,000, some even more than $250,000 and a few even more than $1,000,000.

Question is: who is rich and at the same time crazy enough to wear a small piece of conventional mechanical tech for that kind of money on his wrist? Most people buy houses for that kind of money.

The answer is rather simple: like other works of art, these kind of watches are not in the first place ways to find out what time it is, but ways to store your money in a more lasting kind of investment than currency on a banking account.

However, not every watch brand is suitable as such a form of investment. If you consider investing in a watch (or several watches) the most important rule is the same like with any other form of investment: do not loose your money! So you need a brand or at least a watch model that keeps its value over time. And the list of brands who are capable of that is quite short: these are

1. Rolex

2. Patek Phillippe

3. Omega (some models)

And that's it. The list is quite short. All others loose their value over days, months or at least years. These two consistently hold and in some cases even increase their value over the years.

But these manufacturers are not in that outstanding position for no particular reason: Rolex has a great heritage of technological innovations, like the first automatic watch and the first diving watch. Edmund Hillary wore a Rolex climbing the Mount Everest and the first James Bond watch (Sean Connery wore a Sub in the first James Bond movies) was also a Rolex.

Additionally, Rolex movements are considered very robust. The lore tells us that the only thing that survives a plane crash and is still working, is a Rolex. If your ship sinks and you find your Rolex years later on the seabed, just wind it, it'll still work. You don't purchase a Rolex for just yourself but also for generations to come. All that is marketing nonsense, but there is some truth in it also.

Also adding up to Rolex's reputation is the fact that Rolex builds the whole watch from the ground up completely by themselves. They literally purchase raw steel and raw gold and even create their own Rolex steel-alloy in their own labs. Everything a Rolex watch is, is created by Rolex and nobody else.

To sum it up: Rolex' reputation is based on reliability, robustness, indestructibility, not on luxury and exclusivity in the first place.

Patek Philippe on the contrary does not make so robust watches. You would not go swimming with your Patek, as you wouldn't try to win the Ralley Monte Carlo with your Rolls Royce. Patek is more renown for its outstanding refinement and it's beauty, it's timeless style and elegance and its aristocratic stance. Every surface, every part of the watch, even the movement on the inside is manufactured to absolute perfection. So Patek's reputation is based on brilliance and perfection and luxury and perfect looks. In that sense it is a bit the counterpart of Rolex. Rolex is a new (at least in terms of watchmakers), aggressive and modern manufacturer, Patek is the grandsenior of the watch world. They invented the crown to wind a watch back in the 1800s. I think that alone says a lot.

These are the two brands you can use as an investment alternative to say, gold, art, old-timer cars or what else you like. And in our times it's probably a better investment than in the US-Dollar or the Euro.

For sure there is no rule without exception: Some models made by Omega are interesting for collectors and investors like the Omega Seamaster Professional or the Speedmaster Moonwatch.

And lately a Panerai from the 1950s was sold for $200,000 at an auction. But this is the exception to the rule. If you want to be on the save side of the game you now know what to buy. And basically that old Panerai reached that price, because it is a Rolex. But that is another story.

Buy Today or Cry Tomorrow

This is good advice. The stable or even increasing prices of the top swiss watch brands is on one hand based on the quality and endurance of the watches themselves but also on a second fact: prices in the pricelists of the watchmakers increase every year. And not by little amounts. So good advice to each potential buyer is to buy today, because if you buy tomorrow you will regret it, if you look at the money you'll pay then.

Watch aficionados cry when they see the price lists of the 1990s,

the 1980s or the 1970s, when a Rolex Daytona was $500 – today
it is $10,000 for a new one. Of course this includes inflation, but
some models of the Daytona from that early era went from $500
straight to $100,000 today (no, there are not too many zeros in
that number per accident).

Steel or Gold

If you think about watches as a means of storing capital, the
question might arise, what is better? Steel or gold.

And the first shot is obvious: if you can afford it, a massive
gold watch is at least worth its weight in gold. A steel watch on the
other hand is basically not much more than a very sophisticated
piece of iron.

But think again. It is not only material and workmanship we
are talking about but a market and what the players in that market
think about the pieces.

Let's look at an example: without any doubt it is very attractive
if you, if you're very lucky, have a gold Daytona from 1970 and
offer it for the kind of market price of around $100,000. But how
many potential buyers are there on the planet for that kind of
watch? And how will you – just on he practical side – arrange this
kind of transaction if your buyer lives, let's say, somewhere else on
the planet?

It seems, that it would be much easier to sell 10 steel watches
for $10,000 each than one gold piece for that crazy $100,000. And
there is more: if you diversify, like you will probably have not 10
pieces of the same model, you will also be able to damp losses by
earnings with other models. If nobody wants your 50 year old gold
Daytona anymore you're just screwed. With 10 steel pieces you
will probably always find a buyer.

That's probably why in sum the steel models (and not only
the steel Daytonas) are much more expensive compared to their
real value (basically iron vs. gold). Some steel watches indeed cost
nearly as much as some massiv gold specimen.

Perhaps, if it is not a real lot of money you want to invest in luxury watches, the steel versions seem to be the better alternative, simply because of the huge market there is for them worldwide.

Basically, as I stated above, the steel luxury watch is probably the only real luxury good that is available in a price range that nearly everybody (living in the first world that is) could afford one. The market for them is huge.

Part 3

The Watches

What all these watches have in common is, as we found out, not exactly and not only their ridiculously high price. They have in common that you cannot see their magnificence on a picture. You at least have to see them, better hold them in your hands, best, put them on your wrist where they belong. Believe me, even if you find them like 'ok' on a photo, you have to see them in reality to decide if you like them or not.

3.1 What are Seriously Cool Watches?

Although there are thousands of designs, there is only a hand full of watches that are really cool and can be considered as classics or the cornerstones of watchmaking.

Here again is a lot of subjectivity involved – although I believe that everyone recognizes real class when he sees it. You immediately recognize, if something is a perfect work of art, or just plainly silly. You simply see it intuitively, if every little detail is perfect. You intuitively feel that all the proportions are perfect, that everything is aligned perfectly, that every part of the design resonates with every other part. And that is what these watches are meant to be in their essence: perfect.

On the other hand, there is another aspect to watches: every type of watch has its archetype. Often this is the watch that started something new, that invented something, became the first top seller in a new market, or just was stunningly perfect from day one of its existence.

It also often happens that a watch has the reputation to have started a whole new market, but in truth there was another one before it, that just never became famous. That's the way things go. The perfect one will be remembered forever, the first one is forgotten. It is often not a bad move to purchase the original one, the one that wasn't first but is remembered, the icon. It is not wise to buy the copy of that icon from another watchmaker. It's often not easy to see which is the iconic one. Look for it. We will try to give you an idea on the following pages.

3.2 Do you Really Need That?

Hell Yes!

Something you will always hear from other people, if you wear an expensive luxury watch is the, ›do you need that?‹ question, especially if you wear real tool watches that have special abilities – besides being ridiculously expensive.

If you wear e.g. a diving watch like the Rolex Sea-Dweller, you will hear, that you never even go swimming, what you then need a watch for that can dive 1200 m into the deep. If you wear a racing watch, like the Rolex Daytona, you hear that you never go on a race track with a racing car as you don't have one. If you wear a pilot's watch like the Breitling Transocean you hear that you don't even have a pilot's licence. And if someone has a little wit, he will ask you why you wear a Omega Speedmaster Moonwatch, if you are not a bloody astronaut at all.

The answer to all these – basically rhetorical – questions is always the same: luxury is abundance. Luxury is, when you own something that you don't really need, but fancy. Luxury is to not have to, but could. Luxury is connecting yourself to perfection. And these watches represent perfection in their field.

And sometimes such a show off quality as a pressure resistance to 4000 ft means something quite simple but quite handy: if water cannot enter the case, dust cannot either. And that is really important for a mechanical watch to be resistant to dust – even if that sells worse than ›water resistance‹.

If your watch has a chronograph complication you do not necessarily need to stop the lap time of racing cars. It also can help you timing your tea or your son running the 100 m dash.

So if you consider buying a cool luxury watch, try some of the following watches on your wrist and find out if they fit what you need and expect. That is the most important discipline of all: it has to fit your wrist and feel comfortable on it. You have to like it from the start, you should want it ever since you first saw it. Then it's the right watch for you.

But don't forget: understanding class and style needs some experience as well. You do not necessarily have that from the start. Give it some time to develop.

3.3 Market Structure

The luxury watch world can be separated into three main groups. First is the so called Holy Trinity, the absolute top brands and companies that make, according to the majority of watch enthusiasts the finest watches in the world: Patek-Philippe (PP), Audemars-Piguet (AP) and Vacheron-Constantin (VC).

Next up is the group of Haute Horologie, companies with outstanding historical and technological achievements, like Jaeger-LeCoultre, A. Lange, Breguet and perhaps Blancpain.

And finally there is the heart and core of the luxury watch segment: Rolex, Omega, Breitling and perhaps Panerai and Hublot.

A little Comparison

In order to understand the roles of the top watch manufacturers in the watch market better and perhaps to get them memorized easier, it might help a bit to find parallels of the brands to the much broader known car market. So let's try this:

Holy Trinity

Patek Phillippe = Rolls Royce is expensive from a to z and completely untouchable. Even if they made not the best of the best product, they would still be considered top notch and of highest blood. A holy cow.

Audemars Piguet = Ferrari is provocation and performance in essence. An AP is big, bold, brillant, expensive and not to overlook at all. For AP money is not an issue and also must not be for the owner.

Vacheron Constantin = Aston Martin is much more distinguished than AP but also much more ignored by the market. VC does everything right for the luxury segment but fails a bit to get recognized as much as they would deserve.

Luxury

Rolex = Porsche is loud, dominant, exquisit and cult. No other brand combines technical excellence, focus on the things that really matter and very very long lasting design ideas more than of course Rolex. And all that for a really well balanced price.

Jeager-Lecoultre = Jaguar is avant garde in many ways. JLC's design ideas are Art Deco and Bauhaus. Reduced to the necessary, but utterly beautiful. And they come from a huge tradition of movement making and thus are also superior on the technical side.

Hublot = Lamborghini is blunt, brutal, provoking and aggressive, a little more shine than is actually there. Under the hood is often conventional technology but beautifully reworked. They sport that kind of provocation that made Rolex in ancient times great.

Breguet = Bentley was once the most influential and advanced brand in horology. But things change and although technically brillant, Breguet got overtaken by the young and wild.

IWC = Lotus is pure engineering. A little to puristic, a little too technical, however still a little too conventional – for my taste at least.

Panerai = Maserati is the Italian gentleman in the watch business. It's design is strictly yesterdays but it has lots of style even if the technical aspects are not always outstanding.

Others of Luxury

Omega = BMW is technology, design and price, well in balance. Everything they do, they do brillant. But because they do so much, sometimes they miss their goal anyway.

Breitling = Mercedes is overrated. Charging money like Rolex but delivering only technology of the shelf. And the shouting design often is just too much noise for too less stance.

Tag Heuer = Audi wants to be more than there is. Heuer was once a relevant brand – very much like 'Horch' was in the Audi-comparison – but today they just offer home cooking for a premium price.

3.4   Holy Trinity

Everyone can afford a Rolex. Or a Omega or a Breitling. They are much less than a car. Not so the Holy Trinity watchmakers. These watches are *at least* as much as a decent car, some even cost more than a decent house.

Patek-Philippe Calatrava

The Calatrava is a classic... no, not only: it's the absolute classic dress watch there is. And all the others just copy it. In contrast to all the sports watches, it is most elegant and distinguished. And Patek basically makes it since the early 1930s.

Figure 3.1: Patek-Philippe Calatrava

To be honest I'm not much into dress watches, as most of them are way too subtle for my taste and my wrist. The Calatrava e.g. comes in a 38 mm casing with only 8 mm hight. This is quite subtle, quite decent. It does not make any fuzz about itself. And even the quite formal writing 'Patek Phillipe' on the dial, with no fancy letters, not even a company logo, just tells you what kind of watch you are dealing with – if you are into watches and have heard of the brand before.

However I personally prefer the Porsche attitude of the Rolex sports models. But one has to appreciate that the Calatrava is a fantastically beautiful watch to own.

What's more is that the Calatrava is only available in whitegold, gold and rosegold and no model is below $30,000. But it is definitely the dresswatch to have.

Patek-Philippe Nautilus

Next is another icon of watchmaking: it is one of the finest and most beautiful and at the same time most individual and iconic watches ever conceived:

Figure 3.2: JPatek-Philippe Nautilus

As every watch from Patek, the Nautilus is absolutely perfect in design an stunning in every detail. It simply doesn't get any better than that.

Concerning its design, it obviously is Patek's reaction to AP's sacrilegious and radically modern ›Royal Oak‹ and was even conceived by the same designer.

The only drawback: a Nautilus costs you at least $30,000.

Audemars-Piguet Royal Oak Chronograph

And here is the classic from AP: Made by the same designer as
the Nautilus from Patek, the ›Royal Oak‹ is an icon of watchmaking and watchmaking history and should be part of any serious
collection.

Figure 3.3: Audemars-Piguet Royal Oak Chronograph

The Royal Oak theme over the years has led to many quite
different watches that all share the same key design elements, like
the octogonal bezel and the structured dial. However, the classic
Royal Oak, the Jumbo, the chronograph and later the Offshore
and the Offshore Diver are quite different watches. The latter tend
to look downright threatening and machine-like big. The truth
seems to be: you don't wear a Royal Oak Offshore – it wears you.

Famous for being the first luxury watch made from steel, the
Royal Oak Chrono is about $20,000.

Vacheron Constantin Overseas Chronograph

It's easy to overlook Vacheron Constantin because of their really conservative standing. While Patek is the crown jewel of high horology and AP plays the role of the provocative enfant terrible with their most famous sporty and provokingly large Royal Oak Offshore series, Vacheron is a bit the pale third on a party of two. But they also have their jewels to offer.

Figure 3.4: Audemars-Piguet Royal Oak Chronograph

And conservative with VC means, a history of over 260 years of independent watchmaking. That is a history most other companies cannot compare to. Not even in Swiss watchmaking, where the top dog Rolex still is not more than 120 years old and Hublot not more than 40.

Looking for sporty chronographs it's easy to overlook the Vacheron Constantin Overseas series. And when you find it, of course merely pictures of it at first, because if Patek and AP are scarce VC nearly isn't there at all, then you probably at the first and second glance will find it rather conservative, not to say a bit boring.

Fact is: this watch does not try to be cool or trendy or modern. It is a timeless piece of precision engineering.

But that is until you see it in reality. Then the true beauty of this high horology watch hits you like a hammer. It has the same classy style as a Rolex Submariner oder Sea-Dweller has, it is proportioned perfectly and the attention to detail is as outstanding as you would expect from a member of the holy trinity.

Even the price is as being expected for a holy trinity watch: $20.000.

3.5 High Horology

Along with the holy trinity, there are several watchmakers that make watches at nearly the same level of perfection and precision. But they do not have the same reputation as PP, AP and VC, god knows why. And even if you can tell the difference wearing a magnifying glass and being a full educated watchmaker yourself, as an amateur also these watches will look like absolute perfection to you – because they are.

A. Lange & Söhne Zeitwerk

A. Lange is not a Swiss company but a German one. So what has
this watch to do with the Swiss luxury watches, we discuss here?
A lot.

Figure 3.5: A. Lange Zeitwerk

First of all, this watch is $75,000 – what doesn't make it a
luxury watch as we understand luxury here, but gives an indication
what kind of fellow we are facing.

The Zeitwerk (german meaning 'time-works') is a unique watch.
With its steampunk design, like it came right out of the Fritz
Lang movie ›Metropolis‹, it is somehow the marriage of analog
and digital times.

But there is much more to it. The radically different way of
telling the time requires even radially different techniques and tricks
inside the still completely analog mechanically working movement.

This watch is a design icon and a technological wonder of
watchmaking. At so is the price.

Jaeger-LeCoultre Master Compressor Deep Sea

The Jaeger-LeCoultre Master Compressor Deep Sea Chronograph is very decent. And according to its name it lives in a niche of a niche of a niche.

Figure 3.6: Jaeger-LeCoultre Master Compressor Deep Sea (Ref. 2068570)

But it's true: if you want to have a real luxury watch, you also need at least one watch from a manufacturer, you even cannot pronounce the name of properly. A name nobody but the watch afficionado knows. Companies like Audemars Piguet, Patek Phillippe or Jaeger-LeCoultre.

Jaeger-LeCoultre simply isn't the first watchmaker you think of when it comes to Swiss made luxury watches. They suffer from a rather diffuse image, while in truth they should be famous for their exquisit inhouse movements and the many technical innovations they made in their long history.

And the same way AP is first and foremost famous for its Royal Oak – and today not so very much else – JLC is associated with the Reverso. A model from the 1930s. All that doesn't sound like much.

But while AP followed stricktly the market focussing on their
primary success and today makes dozens of variations of the Royal
Oak theme, so many that they easily could change their company
name to 'Royal Oaks A.S.' (what everybody could memorize much
easier), JLC still has a lot of different cool watches that don't
have anything to do with the Reverso. E.g. the great Master
Compressor diving watch series.

The Master Compressor also in technical terms is so good that
some years ago JLC and not Rolex or Omega got the order from
the Navy Seals to create a diving watch for their special forces
based on the Master Compressor series. And the result was a
rugged military grade tool watch that soldiers in combat can rely
on – not just a present for veterans.

The Master Compressor Deep Sea on the other hand is also a
serious diving watch, but primarily a homage to a vintage model
from the 1950s. That is of course not per accident in these times
of vintage model craziness.

However, the great design of the Deep Sea is another proof
that there are indeed timeless designs that are as great today as
they were 50 years ago. And timelessness is the key to it keeping
its value, remember?

And the Deep Sea is still a proper diving watch and it's not
worth a mention that this one is of course $10,000.

What I personally don't like about the Deep Sea is the strap.
Of course it is high quality and wears extremely comfortable. But
there is a problem: leather straps tend to age. If you wear them
on a daily basis after 2 to 5 years they do not look like a new one
at all. You either have to replace it or they tend to look more and
more ugly.

You of course can get the Deep Sea with a steel bracelet. But
this does not look so nice as the black leather strap. It changes the
character of the watch a lot. The solution would of course be to
get the watch with two straps. One for wearing and one for having
a full set of the watch with the original unworn strap for keeping
up the resale price of your piece. But who does that kind of thing

as I estimate the strap will be at least $300?

3.6   Luxury

What the Holy Trinity watchmakers are for Haute Horologie the
Luxury Holy Trinity is for the rest: Rolex, Omega and Breitling.
These three really *own* the luxury watch market. They offer
brillantly made, robust and stylish luxury watches that are worth
the money.

Rolex GMT Master II

The probably most famous Rolex watch of all ist the GMT Master II with the ›Pepsi‹ bezel.

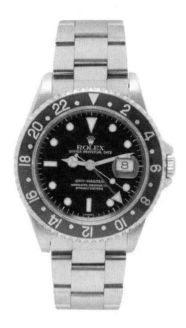

Figure 3.7: Rolex GMT Master II

Compared to a lot of other watches that can look quite similar to each other, the GMT Master II with the ›Pepsi‹ bezel is most recognizable. And I has a great track record.

Starting out with Goldfingers Pilot ›Pussy Galore‹ in the James Bond movie, the GMT II became one of the must have watches of the 1980s and 1990s. Tom ›Magnum‹ Selleck wore one driving his Ferrari around Hawaii, all the Formula 1 drivers and managers up to Nikki Lauda and Luca de Montezemolo also have one and wear them quite proudly a lot.

The GMT Master was originally designed by Rolex to have a watch with two separate Timezones for pilots and other people that change timezones a lot. But I doubt that most GMT owners bought this watch for that reason.

However, today the retail version from Rolex is only available as a whitegold ceramic bezel version for around $30,000.

And the thing with the new GMT Master II is this: Although you might have overlooked it at the first glance, Rolex changed the design of the GMT Master II in 2008 more than with all renovations between 1954 and 2008 combined.

The new ceramic six-digit reference GMT got the new Rolex super case and the maxi dial and the creamic bezel – and the new Oyster bracelet with all massive links. And that altogether changed the appearence, the look and feel of the GMT massively – and, like many say, into the wrong direction. Don't get me wrong: the ceramic bezel is a great thing concerning durability. The solid bracelet gives the watch a much more valuable feel. But the super case is just too large for a watch like that. The super case works perfect with the Seadweller 4000 (116600), but with the GMT it's simply too large.

The former model, the 16710 was a very subtle watch with an elegant case, a beautiful bezel with elegant numbers for the 24-hours hand on it, a very very light (hollow links) bracelet. It was very comfortable to wear.

The new one tends to be bloated, a case on steroids, a hefty bracelet and a visually too dominant bezel with very agressively designed numbers. It tends to wear heavy, stands up against the wrist and is quite dominant. It became more an oversized sports watch than an elegant and unobtrusive tool watch for business people that jet around the world.

That's why a lot of people prefer the older 16710 over the new 116710.

Unfortunately the 16710 is of course discontinued since 2008 and constantly out of stock. The supply of used watches is also quite limited what makes the prices go up. And the last model with the all new 3186 movement is quite sought for. For a NOS one you can easily invest $20,000 or more. Even if it's a literally more than 10 years old watch.

Rolex Sea Dweller

Most watch experts consider the Rolex Submariner being the most important and most iconic watch on the planet. That might be true. However on the other hand, a luxury watch is something that impresses also by scarcity – and that important quality meanwhile the Sub fails a bit, because really ›everybody has one‹ – ok, that is: everybody who's even slightly interested in watches and has the money to run around with a $5,000 piece on the wrist.

Figure 3.8: Rolex Sea Dweller (Ref. 16600)

So in my opinion the number one position in luxury watches should be meanwhile taken by the Rolex Sea-Dweller, a kind of improved next step Submariner. It has all that the Sub ever was, but is better and more exclusive as well. It's more modern, it can dive down to 4000 ft, it lacks the ›cyclops‹ lense over the date window that is haunting most Rolex sapphire crystal designs and it is at the sweet spot of all watch case diameters: 40 mm with a acceptable and masculine height of 15 mm. In one word: it is the perfect watch from the perfectionist watchmaker No.1.

It is simply one of the greatest sports watches you can buy for money. And with $9,000 it is not too expensive at all.

But don't confuse this Sea-Dweller it with the Sea-Dweller 'Deep Sea'. The Deep Sea is much bigger and tends to be clunky and less comfortable to wear. For some years the Sea-Dweller was completely replaced by the Sea-Dweller 'Deep Sea' that has a modern, hulking 44 mm case with a hight of unbelievable 18 mm, that for most wrists is simply way too big to be worn with comfort. That thickness is technically necessary partly, because it is water proof to a depth of 12,000 ft.

However Rolex heard the call of the customers who wanted the traditional Sea Dweller back with its much more wearable and much less massive 40 mm case. And so Rolex finally brought the 40 mm Sea-Dweller back at the Baselworld watch fair in 2013 with the Sea-Dweller 4000 with the modern ceramic bezel. Kind of the wearable brother of the extreme Deep Sea.

The Sea-Dweller is very much like the Submariner a classic Rolex dive watch. Black dial, black bezel, steel case, steel bracelet. And it's a serious diver's watch as well as it is waterproof down to 4000 ft, 1200 m. It is even more masculine than the Sub and thus a little more modern. Compared to other diving watches, that are often quite rugged it has a subtle luxury as e.g. the markings on the dial are white-gold. If you ever had one on your wrist you instantly feel and see the difference to other ›lesser‹ watches. A feeling of perfection, precision and luxury that clearly and profoundly divides it from even aspiring watchmakers like Omega, Breitling or Tag-Heuer. You instantly feel, why a Rolex is a rather different beast.

And there is more. The heart of the Sea-Dweller, the Rolex 3135 movement is considered one of the best movements ever made. That means, it is a perfect combination of accuracy, reliability and robustness. It might not be the most beautiful movement or the most refined. But if you want your watch to give you the exact time under any circumstances imaginable, the 3135 movement will not let you down.

And one single fact may illustrate, how far Rolex goes, when it comes to accuracy: even the Sea-Dweller has some inaccuracies. Depending on the position you are putting it down when you go to bed, it will show the wrong time of about -12 to +6 seconds per day – if you ever put it down...

But this is not the whole truth, it's even the wrong measurement. If you wear it, and that is what the watch is meant for, this not so spectacularly good error value is reduced to an inaccuracy of 2 seconds per week (!). And that is, because all the moving parts of the movement are optimized to work at body temperature. When the watch is on your arm it acquires your body temperature. And as all metal parts will expand or shrink depending on their temperature, there is an ideal temperature at which the movement runs best. And that is body temperature.

Rolex Submariner (nodate)

Still, you cannot avoid the Submariner. And as I am (for estetic reasons) one of the cyclops-lens-haters (the lens over the date window), in my opinion the no-date version of the Submariner is the sweet spot.

Figure 3.9: Rolex Submainer (nodate) (Ref. 114060)

The Sub is recognized as the most important sports watch ever. Of course because the predecessor for today's model was one of the first diving watches and of course because Sean Connery as James Bond 007 wore a Sub in all the iconic first Bond movies. Probably the last fact is more important than all the others.

The Sub comes in two versions: with a date window with cyclops lens and without date (and so of course without the cyclops). And being a real toolwatch the Sub is perfectly suited in steel. But it is also available in gold which you should take into consideration if you a) like the yellow metal on your wrist and it fits your style and b) if you see the watch as a financial investment into something of lasting value.

In its classic steel incarnation the Sub is a serious diver's watch, but it's also a dress-watch, it can be worn everywhere and always makes a good figure.

Yes Rolex makes their own steel only for their watches. And that makes sense. Not only suffer watches, especially the highly polished and finished luxury watches from scratches. That alone would make it a good thing to have a hard and scratch resistant steel. No. The Rolex 904L steel has also an improved resistance against sea water, salt water. Perfect for dive-watches like the Submariner, Sea Dweller or Yacht Master. Right?

But... ok..., you will never dive with your Rolex? You will take it of before you enter the shower? But doesn't that make that whole steel-thing an utter nonsense?

Basically it's the same as with the water-tightness of 100 and more meters. This is in 99 of 100 cases not necessary, as most Rolex buyers will never dive to more than 30 m and most not even this deep, because they don't have a bathtub that's 30 m deep. But think about it: a watch case that is absolutely tight against water is also tight against dust. And this is an everyday problem for a mechanical watch. Dust-tightness is essential.

It's the same thing with the steel. Even if you never go diving into the sea, you constantly confront your watch with salt-water: sweat. Sweat also is salty water and rather similar to sea-water. So a case that resists the salty sea-water better will also be more resistant against the chemical challange of everyday sweat.

However this all only applies if you take your Rolex out of your safe, what you definitely should.

Omega Seamaster Professional

Also featuring a brillant design is the next watch that was the official James Bond watch of the early 2000s: the Omega Seamaster Professional.

Figure 3.10: Omega Seamaster Professional

The Seamaster series is the iconic diving watch along with the Rolex Submariner. Some even say it was Omega who invented the serious diving watches with the Ploprof. Earlier models were just waterproof.

May that be as it is. The Seamaster Professional with its blue bezel and blue structured dial is going to be one of the alltime perfect classics.

But this model was not only worn by James Bond. It has a very high quality and beautiful bracelet, an excellent clasp and a beautiful dial and bezel. And with that DNA it seriously attacked the rivaling Rolex models in quality and design. So this watch has a very important historic aspect: it is said that these features combined with its outstanding success on the market forced Rolex to develop all the changes to their models we today really value: the new Oyster bracelet with its solid links, the brillant Oyster clasp and the nearly indestructible ceramic bezels.

The Seamaster Professional is not only a significant watch for Omega as it helped Omega to reinvent the Seamaster brand, it also had a huge impact on the whole market especially on Rolex and the quality they offer.

It's the only watch in the list that is only available as a vintage piece. In the late 1990s it cost about $1,500, but today these models are at least $3,000 on the market.

Rolex Cosmograph 'Daytona'

One of the most wanted and least available watches on the market is the Rolex Daytona in steel. If you want to purchase one, it may easily happen that the dealer tells you that you will have to wait some 8 to 10 years (!) to get one.

Figure 3.11: Rolex Cosmograph 'Daytona' Ref. 116520

The Daytona is just a beauty. Some might find the steel version with the white dial less masculine than the black dial version. But in my opinion the white dial and the steel bezel are the two main characteristics of the Daytona. The ceramic bezel makes it a bit undistinguished. And for around $10,000 the Daytona is not really expensive, as funny as this might sound.

The Daytona Effect: Not long ago I saw a Rolex Daytona from 1973. 18k Gold. And the seller also attached the original pricelist of 1973. Remember in 1973 a Mercedes E-Class was roughly about $15000. The Gold Daytona was around $3000. Today a Daytona of that kind in good condition sells for $95000. Don't ask what you get for the 1973 E-Class. The same thing applies to Rolex

Submariners from that decade.

The 10 Years Myth

There is the myth. And it says, that you occasionally have to wait about 10 years if you want to buy a new Rolex Cosmograph 'Daytona' from a Rolex 'Konzessionär', meaning an official Rolex dealer that is certified by Rolex to sell their products.

If you go to any Rolex Konzessionär today you will eventually hear this story. »Oh yes, we have a waiting list for the steel Daytona models and perhaps, if you are very lucky, you will be able to get one in less than 9 years from now.« But only if you're lucky.

So far the myth. What is this story about? Who is making a watch that he could sell thousands of, but only makes hundreds of them? Are these Swiss guys crazy?

If you go to one of the major internet portals where dealers all over the world sell their watches, new and pre-owned, you find, not exactly lots of, but you are able to find a new steel Daytona lets say within 100 km around you – if you don't happen to live in the middle of the Sahara desert. So where does this myth come from, because obviously the 10-year-waiting-list is just that?

Truth is: the Daytona *was* rare. In the 1990s when Rolex decided to use a Zenith movement in their Daytona models, the Daytona got rare, because Zenith is a rather small company and could not produce enough movements to fit their own chronograph, the Zenith 'El Primero' as well as the Rolex Daytona with them in the quantities that giant Rolex needed.

So to this day the Daytona with the Zenith movement is somewhat rare, very good and for that combination of reasons sought for.

However, today this problem of low production quantities of the Daytona is history as the Daytona since the late 1990s uses the Rolex inhouse movement that Rolex is able to supply in quantities sufficient for the Daytona. But the legend is kept alive and the Daytona is said to be very rare. That makes it more interesting and distinguishes it from other legends like the Omega Speedmaster Moonwatch.

Rolex Yacht-Master

At the end of the 1980, Rolex realized that they were not only a premium brand selling tool-watches, but – after 90 years of excellent watchmaking – they became primarily a premium brand. So they discussed the possibilities to give their flagship, the Submariner a more luxurious design.

Figure 3.12: Rolex Yacht-Master (Ref. 116622)

The result was the Yacht-Master. Obviously in the end they did not dare to change the look of the Sub so radically, but also liked the platinum design of the Yacht-Master so much that they did not replace the Sub but created an new product line. And this happens less often than the pope changes.

The Yacht-Master wears extremely comfortable. And it is pure pleasure every time you look at it. Of course its readability varies from good down to very poor depending on the light situation. But anyway if you wear your Rolex only to find out the time you missed out something for crying out loud.

The Yacht-Master is about $12.000 and a really unconventional but extremely pretty timepiece and will definitely become one of the all time classics.

Omega Speedmaster Professional

There is no necessity to say a lot about this watch. The marketing mega-deal of the century went to Omega.

Figure 3.13: Omega Speedmaster Professional

They were able to supply the watch that the astronauts wore, who went to the moon. Men like Armstrong, Aldrin, Collins and all the others not only got an Omega Speedmaster, they literally wore it on their astronauts suit while landing and walking on the moon.

This is a watch that was worn by the men who flew to the moon, right? And this watch is manual wind, right? What the heck? Was it rocket science to at least give it an automatic movement? Of course a watch used in space is manual wind. Why? Think about it: The men who flew to the moon experienced microgravity. Most of the time, more than 7 days during their flight there and back was nearly no gravity at all. Everything floats up there. How on gods good green earth should an automatic movement work, if there is no gravity that pulls the anchor of the movement towards a gravitational center, like e.g. the earth's relative to the movement of the wearer?

The key to understand this is: in space, an automatic movement does not self wind. It cannot, because it needs gravity as the source of energy it uses to self wind. The questions is: what force should move the rotor that propels an automatic winding mechanism? And the answer is: there is none. So it makes completely no sense to build a space watch with an automatic movement, so this watch must be manual wind.

So you can as well use a manual winding movement, and that is exactly what Omega and the NASA did. It just makes sense.

What really astonished me and what is proof that this cooperation between Omega and the NASA is more than just a marketing gag, is the fact that the Speedmaster story was not finished after the first Moon landing, not even after the end of the Apollo Moon Program. Even in recent years the Speedmaster Professional was part of the Space Shuttle missions and was used in the space walks outside the spaceship.

So if you fancy a real exclusive watch with an outstanding story, the Speedmaster is right for you. In my eyes it has not the perfect beauty of a Rolex Daytona, because it is too black for my eyes, with the black dial and the black bezel. But it is still one of the most important watches in watchmaking history. And it is quite cheap for $4,000.

Panerai Luminor Marina PAM111

This is a watch that is ›impossibile‹: a watchmaker that started out being a Swiss watch from Italy and – as manufacturing completely moved from Italy to Switzerland – being today an Italian watch from Switzerland. Panerai.

Figure 3.14: Panerai Luminor Marina (Ref. PAM00111)

Early Panerai watches even had Rolex movements, so even in the early days they always have been something special. And Panerai is an old company. It was started in Florence, Italy in the early 1850s. So even if Panerai watches became en vogue within the last 10 years or so, they have a long history, tradition and heritage.

And there is more to the Rolex-Panerai connection of the early years that meets the eye. Rolex began in the 1930s to develop a diving watch which eventually much later ended in the Submariner. However at first the design was a 47 mm oversized waterproof watch that did not do quite well and was discontinued before it could take off.

At the same time Panerai in Italy, who built Rolex movements in their watches, were looking for a diving watch design and came up with a large oversized watch rather similar to the discontinued Rolex design. So the oversized Panerai divers like at first the Radiomir and from there the Luminor originally stem back from a Rolex design.

Then, when Panerai showed that there was indeed a significant market for diving watches, Rolex again put some effort into development of a professional diving watch and in 1953 presented the Submariner, eventually becoming the best, most iconic and most respected diving watch of all time. While the original Panerai design is also still around in its incarnation of the modern Radiomir and Luminor models.

What makes Panerai even more outstanding is that it is built in the same design as they started out more than 60 years ago and it has a manual wind movement. So this is really a watch for the watch enthusiast, as it takes some care to wind it every two or three days to work properly. It is a watch for having a close relationship to. The PAM111 is 44 mm in diameter at a height of 15 mm. It is a watch with presence, a real piece to wear, not just a way to know what time it is. And you can get this beauty for only $6,000.

The Panerai Luminor models are big. With 44 mm cases they sit comfortably on the wrist but undoubtedly with presence. They are watches for the watch enthusiast, who wears a watch not only to guess time, but very conscious, as a special kind of techno-jewelry. In the case of the Luminor, as a kind of furniture. It's a part of your lifestyle not just a tool to know what time it is.

The Panerai Luminor design has some of that italian mojo. It is blunt, not to say brutal, like a military watch has to be. But it also is elegant, so you can easily pull it off with a shirt and a suit. At least as a contrapunctus to the overall elegance of the suit. On the wrist it feels manly and also comfy. It is beautiful and rugged, masculine and subtle all at the same time. It is, what makes a classic.

The Panerai Luminor watches that are swiss made since 1993,

started the vintage watch trend. Since their success story took off a lot of other watchmakers started vintage style models and the real old watches became dramatically sought of and expensive.

There is another watch that demands this style of big and bold but stylish more than many others: the Hublot Big Bang. It is also large, it is a piece of art that takes the AP Royal Oak idea and improves it far beyond – at least in style. And it is also a watch for the enthusiast, as you cannot wear a Big Bang without noticing or being noticed.

So I'd put it that way: for me the 1950s Luminor design is sort of the Big Bang of the 50s. It wears like it, it has the same kind of uncompromising presence. And it also is a true beauty.

But you may say: man, this is a manual winding watch. It has no automatic movement, what means, even if you wear it all day, you have to wind it. Yes, that's correct. You have to wind it every two days, because it has a power reserve of 3 days when it's fully wound. And yes, this is not state of the art in mechanical watches, at least not since Rolex introduced the 'perpetual' automatic movement to the mass market somewhere back in the 1940s.

And I will not argue that this is ok, because it is kind of a vintage watch. No. What you experience when you wear a PAM111 is that the manual wind gives you something you won't expect: not only a deeper and more personal connection to your watch but first and foremost: control. You know, when it is fully wound and you know that this will suffice for another 56 hours. And that is appropriate for a military tool watch. You always need to be sure that it shows the right time.

That is also the case why I prefer the PAM111 over the PAM112 that misses the small second display at 9 o'clock. Because a watch is worth it's price if it has a bundle of features that together make sense. And the small second makes sense, it is in some respect essential. Not only to get the swiss COSC certificate that says it is highly accurate (for a mechanical watch). No. If you use the watch like it was meant to be, under water, in a military setting, you need to be sure it runs and shows the correct time. Your live might depend on it. The small second is not so much a feature to know the seconds, but to see the watch runs. In my opinion.

If you start collecting luxury watches, you want quintessential watches, you want the icons of a watchmaker, of a type or style first. You don't want to mess with strange designs or irrational bundles of features. You want, what is typical and quintessential.

What is quintessential Panerai? It's in my opinion the sandwich dial (the two layer dial with one layer being the luminosent material and the second layer the dial itself with the hour markers cut out), the patented crown guard, the manual wind movement as it is typical for the Panerai era of the 1930s to 1950s, it is the large Luminor and Radiomir cases and the unusually broad leather straps, the military tool watch style. Simple, elegant, uncompromised, rugged, masculine.

Just one word on the strap: don't be irritated by the light brown strap of the PAM111. Firstly it looks much darker and much more luxurious in reality and secondly, it is one of the Panerai specialities that you can change straps downright in a minute. It is very easy and this propelled a secondary market of all sorts of straps for Panerai watches without parallel in the history of luxury watches. So the sweet spot in Panerai collectors might be, buy a Panerai and buy the strap you like – and keep the original strap in the box, in case you want to sell the watch later as a complete package with the leather strap untouched.

Hublot Big Bang

You love it or you hate it. This is the ultimate fun watch. A design borrowed from the AP Royal Oak and developed much further than a hundreds of years old company like AP could ever imagine. Only Hublot could do something like that, as one of the young and wild watchmakers, the company being only 40 years old.

Figure 3.15: Hublot Big Bang Evo Steel Ceramic

Hublot watches are variations on the classic Royal Oak theme that originally was conceived by AP in the 1970s. Hublot even tried to copy the provocation of the ›Royal Oak‹ of using a lesser material in a luxury watch: AP used steel for the case – and Hublot went for using rubber straps. And it (again) worked. They are not only fancy but beautiful timepieces. This steel/ceramic version is $12,000.

Audemars Piguet also got out their own interpretation of the Royal Oak theme for the modern day, the Royal Oak Offshore. It is obviously an extremely valuable watch. But in my opinion, you won't seriously wear a $20,000 watch in sea-water, will you? So it is a bit of a misunderstanding. And that's why I like the

Hublot interpretation better. It is a fun watch, made of innovative materials you can wear everywhere – primarily above the water. Even if it is not water resistant like a real diving watch should be, although it looks like one. But that is kind of part of the fun it is, the fun it makes of you and all the others.

Maybe Hublot is even the new Rolex of the 21st century. What do I mean by that? Well, Hublot is quite new in the game and amazingly successful. Rolex also was not one of the classic watchmakers like e.g. Vacheron Constantin, Breguet, Patek or even Omega with a history dating back to the 19th or even 18th century. Rolex was founded in 1903 and only slowly became famous after WW I. And how did they do it? By innovation and of course by product placement.

Edmund Hillary wore an early version of the Explorer on the Everest and Sean Connery a Submariner as 007. What more do you need to make a watchmaker cool?

And Rolex stacked invention upon invention, the first waterproof watch (Oyster case), the first automatic watch (Perpetual movement), the first sports luxury watch (the Sub) and so on. Lately the rate of great patents slows down a bit and others take over, hungry for success. Like Hublot.

Hublot experiments a lot with exotic materials, provocative design and ironic products. The rubber strap, scratch resistant ceramic-gold cases, large, not-at-all decent watches. Hublot is recognizable and knows marketing as well as watchmaking. Being founded in 1980 Hublot is a newcomer on the watch Olymp and a little bit an enfant terrible like Rolex was in the early 20th century.

And for more than a decade now their Big Bang series is one of the most stylish and most requested watches on the market. So maybe they just start out to become the 'Rolex' of the 21st century.

3.7 Budget Alternatives

You may say, »this is most interesting, but I don't want to spend like 10 or 20 grand for just a wristwatch. Even if it's a kind of financial investment I just don't have the money for that but still want a great Swiss made luxury watch nevertheless. Which one should I buy in that case?«

Luckily in our recommendations there are some watches with a style that is so iconic that nearly every watchmaker does something similar so you have a lot of choice – and some of them are quite beautiful too. If you fancy a dress watch like the Patek Calatrava, you might also like the Eterna 1948 or the Rolex Datejust II. The same applies for chronographs like the Rolex Daytona and a equally classic but much less pricy Omega Speedmaster.

For some watches you can also get cheaper quartz versions. I would not go for that, because a real swiss watch, even a budget one, has a mechanical movement. That rule sticks even with lower budget luxury watches.

Eterna 1948

Eterna is one of the most successful watchmakers in history. Never heard of them? Oh yes, you have. Eterna is nobody less than ETA, the guys who manufacture the movements for that legion of watchmakers that do not make their own movements.

Figure 3.16: Eterna 1948

So if you buy an Omega, a Breitling, a Tag-Heuer, a Longines, a Oris, a Movado, a Tudor or a Chopard, you basically always buy a Eterna watch (the movement) with a nice and quite individual case.

The other way around, the bottom line is: Eterna sells watches made with their own inhouse movements and thus is a true luxury brand, and not just a designer of fancy cases. The Eterna movements are indeed quite good, reliable, patented and not too expensive, what makes an Eterna watch a real alternative.

The Eterna 1948 is more of a dress watch. It resembles the much more expensive Patek Philippe Calatrava in some way but costs only $2,000. And if you ask me, it is a really beautiful watch.

However at his price point it is not really a luxury watch and by that the rules of luxury goods do not necessarily apply to it.

Rolex Datejust

Rolex divides its market into two sections. One is the sports models like the Sub, the Sea-Dweller, the Daytona, the GMT Master II, the Explorer II with the same movement as the GMT Master II and the Yacht Master. These are sometimes hard to get and are quite expensive.

Figure 3.17: Rolex Datejust (Ref. 116200)

On the other hand there are the Rolex volume models that are easy to get and are a lot cheaper. And all the Rolex models start out with the Oyster Perpetual.

This is a historical thing. The ›Oyster‹ case is the patented Rolex waterproof case. And the ›Perpetual‹ movement is the Rolex automatic wind movement, but it got a special name, as Rolex was the first company to ship automatic movements at a larger scale. So the automatic movement is kind of a trademark of Rolex.

Other models like the Datejust and the Daydate are basically the same watch as the Oyster Perpetual with increasingly complex ›complications‹, what means additional functions, like a date or weekday display.

The 39 mm Explorer as well as the 41 mm Datejust II are more or less somewhere in between these both worlds. It half sports watch and half volume model. And you get quite a lot of Rolex for the money and you can get it quite easily – you perhaps have to wait for one 4-6 weeks – not 4-6 years.

I prefer the Datejust in the plain form. Clean bezel, black dial, Oyster Bracelet, no nonsense. Not even the shiny blue dial, that a lot of people love so much. This classic watch is around $6,000 and worth every penny.

Rolex Explorer

Maybe I am doing the Explorer wrong, but in my eyes it is just a Oyster Perpetual with another dial. But that is not a problem at all. The Explorer did not go to the Moon with Neil Armstrong but it went up to Mount Everest with Edmund Hillary – and that's not so much a difference on your wrist.

Figure 3.18: Rolex Explorer

And the Explorer is not available in a lot of different versions. An Explorer is an Explorer is an Explorer. It only grew in size in the last years from 36 to 39 mm. But in my opinion that's a good thing. The 39 mm is the way to go for the modern man. 36 mm looks too much like a toy or lady's version on the wrist on a grown up man. Even if some aficionados tell you that only the classic one is the real one. In times of 44 and 48 mm watches becoming mainstream, a 36 mm case is a little outdated.

And with the Explorer you get real Rolex DNA, a very versatile watch you can wear on a mountain or in an office that is robust and distinguished at the same time. A lot of Rolex aficionados love the Explorer.

And it is good value for money at a retail price of around $5,500.

Part 4

Important Aspects

Rolex is Cult like Porsche

Obviously one watchmaker is standing out. Like Porsche does in the world of luxury cars.

Mercedes or Rolls Royce?

There are the classic Rolex watches, the volume-models, like the Oyster Perpetual, the Daydate or the Explorer. I personally like them, but not so much as the sports watches.

And that is the case, because in my opinion, to say it in car brand terms, a Rolex is not a Mercedes or a Rolls Royce; a Rolex is a Porsche. So the whole game is that a Rolex watch in my opinion should be not too subtle, it should have a presence, even provoke a bit. A Rolex is not shy or reserved, but sporty and loud. And that's why I like the Rolex sports watches more than the other models.

Rolex has another advantage: if you are new to luxury watches, you will be at least mildly shocked by the prices. Even if you knew that a luxury watch will be thousands of dollars, you might not have expected them to be ten-thousands of dollars. So if you consider buying your first luxury watch, you might want four things to start with:

1. a not too expensive model

2. a model that will not loose its value

3. a versatile model, you can wear with a jeans and a suit

4. a real beauty, you will be proud of

All that brings you to the Rolex Sea-Dweller. Patek only is an option if you easily have $30,000 to spent. Omega is at the moment quite expensive as they want to attack Rolex in their market and they might be able to do so, but still they do not have the reputation for the Rolex-like pricing policy. So Omega at the moment is just quite expensive. Hublot is more a millionaire's toy and the AP Royal Oak also expects a lot from your purse and additionally AP will charge you a lot for technical service of the watch. If you like the 1970s style and are fascinated by the Nautilus you might consider a Patek Philippe Aquanaut. If these watches are too sporty for you, you might want to have a look at the Calatrava.

Rolex Store Windows

Perhaps you sometimes wondered what all the fuzz is about Rolex. When you go to a Rolex store and look in the shop window, there are several Rolex models and they all are downright ugly. One by one you either do not like the large cyclops lens on top of the date window, you do not like the in a strange way reminding of the 1980s case form and as a man of style you of course do not like the application of gold parts, the shimmering dial colors or even the also rather 1980s looking bracelet. Sometimes the bezel also looks like being straight from the 1980s and everything seems a bit like a bonbon showcase for people with a bad taste and obviously too much money.

Well, that is, because the Rolex watches you find in a shop window are usually not the real cool top watches but the ones the dealer has in stock, trying to sell them.

You won't find the Submariner in a window, nor a Sea-Dweller or a Deep Sea, not a Explorer II, rather seldom a GMT Master and of course not a steel Daytona. The cool ones are almost never in stock and the dealer has no need to put them in a window, as he will sell them rather quickly anyway to customers who know what they want and ask for it. Dealers often have waiting lists for these watches.

So, if you are looking for a Rolex watch, do not look into the window, go inside and ask for the cool models, the real cool Rolex models. And put them on your wrist. If you then put another watch like a Breitling or a Tag Heuer or even an Omega on your same wrist, you will immediately know why Rolex watches are a class of their own.

And by the way: also the rather boring models like the Datejust have their own cool style but as I told you: give it some time. Style and the feel for style must develop.

The Real Things

Porsche was characterized by Ferry Porsche (the son of the founder) being a company that builds »cars that nobody needs, but everbody wants«. With Rolex it's a rather similar thing. In my opinion the two brands have a similar standing. Like Porsche a Rolex is not too subtle. It's sporty, it's gripping, it does not care too much about what others think. A Rolex watch may be a little loud, a little overly masculine, a little yesterdays and irrational. But at the same time, and exactly because of that, it's a lot of fun, appealing to a special kind of customer, a celebration of living a life with not too tight financial boundaries and certainly no regrets.

Much the same like Porsche also Rolex is cult. No other brand managed to place so many icons in the market like Rolex did. And that's why everybody knows Rolex. No other brand is so broadly known. Not Patek although they are considered being the absolute number one of fine watchmaking and someday in the past invented something so basic like the crown (to wind the watch), not Breguet although they would deserve it, not Jaeger-LeCoultre although they stack innovation upon innovation, not even Omega, who sell a lot more watches than Rolex. Rolex is King, because their watches are cult. Rolex has only 1% of the watch market, but makes 25% of the money. Most people even think Rolex makes the most expensive watches (not true) and Rolex is the top brand in watchmaking (also not true). But Rolex is still number one in brand recognition.

And there is more: once you had a Rolex on your wrist and you compare it to other watches you often find out: Rolex plays in its own league. The precision alone when you unscrew the crown to wind the movement crushes every ETA movement and with it the largest portion of the watch market. If you rotate the bezel you find out what real precision is. The refinement of every surface is simply outstanding.

The iconic Rolex cult watches are and each of it is worth owning and wearing:

- The Datejust

- The Explorer

- The Submariner

- The GMT Master II

- The Explorer II

- The Daytona

- The Sea-Dweller

- The Yachtmaster

And don't forget: whatever happens, Rolex is an internationally accepted 'currency'. With a Rolex you always wear a cash reserve on your wrist in case you loose everything, you can still buy a ticket home.

If nobody inherits you a Rolex. Don't bother with vintage models pretending to have a Rolex tradition you haven't. Be the founder of the tradition, start it, become the legend, the first one in your family. Be the guy who began purchasing long term value goods.

4.1　Rolex-ology

If you look for Rolex watches on internet plattforms you will encounter a lot of codes and keywords that are often hard to understand for the beginner, as a lot of them have their own history. Here are some of these described, so you can understand where they come from and what they mean...

A...Z Series

If you find a watch that is e.g. described as 'T-Series' that means that its serial number begins with the letter 'T' followed only by digits, eight digits. And if it was made before 2011 this means that this particular watch was made in 1996 or 1997.

And here is why:

From 1927 on until 1987 Rolex gave every watch an individual number. And with this number you could also find out in which year your watch was made, as there are tables available (not by Rolex themselves, of course) that show which numbers were use in which year, roundabout. E.g. if you have a watch with the serial number '698-767' (I inserted the slashes for ease of reading. Rolex does not have these). it should have been made in 1961.

Unfortunately there is a little complication to that rule: in 1954 Rolex already reached watch number 999-999 and they just began to count serial numbers again from 0 in that year. So your watch with the serial number '698-767' also could be from 1950. But concerning the models, 1950 and 1961 should be easily distinguishable.

However, this also means that if your serial number is higher than 1-000-000 your watch is definitely newer than 1964 as Rolex again reached the 999-999 in that year.

Then in 1987 Rolex reached number 9-999-999 and again they changed the system. This time they began to use one letter leading a six-digit serial number. But unfortunately they did not use the letters in their natural sequence but nearly random. They started in 1987 with R (like Rolex, I suppose). Then in 1988 they went to

L, then two years later to E and X. If you miss out the O (letter O) it probably would have looked to much like an 0 (zero) and this could have lead to problems, although Rolex did never mark their watches with serial numbers with a leading zero.

What a pity, because otherwise the first letters from that years would have been R-O-L-E-X. Funny. But this way it was R-L-E-X.

Then came letters N-C-S-W-T-U-A-... and so on following no obvious rule any more. If it is still an acronym, nobody knows its meaning.

So if you read in the description of a watch that it is from a Z-series, that does not mean that this is the final series of that model or something like that but only that it was made during the Z-serial number era and this e.g. was between somewhere in 2006 and somewhere 2007. Rolex also changed the letter not with the year in the calender but just when numbers behind the letter again reached 999-999.

This system obviously was limited to 24 times 999.999 watches. And so the letter system naturally reached its limit in 2011.

Random Series

Since then in 2011 Rolex uses a system of eight letters and numbers that are created randomly. This obviously was easily possible by the use of computers to generate a random number that is not already in the database.

That means also that since 2011 only Rolex knows when a watch was made. The serial number alone gives no clue at all when a watch was built in the Rolex facilities any more.

What you often find in the description of a watch is the word 'Random Series'. That means that the watch has no serial number of that old kind but was made after 2011 and has a serial number that gives no clue how old the watch really is – besides that it was made after 2011, obviously.

LC100

LC means 'Ländercode' german for 'country code'. LC100 e.g. means that the watch was originally delivered to Germany and sold there. Codes lower than LC100 mean that the watch was sold in Switzerland and so on.

An interesting peculiarity is that a lot of military bases have their own LC-number, like LC907 for the NATO headquarters in Germany.

NOS

Very seldom on online watch portals you will encounter a watch that is called 'NOS'. This abbreviation stands for 'New Old Stock'.

That means this watch was made years ago, e.g. in 2005 or 1997 or even 1981, but it was never sold, it was never worn, it is brand new, although it was made some ten, twenty or even more years ago.

And that is why these watches often are two to three times more expensive than their normal 'used' counterparts. NOS is so to say the creme de la creme of vintage watches. An old but virgin watch.

Some 'NOS' or 'near NOS' called watches have been sold but never worn, often they have all the original stickers on them. The main difference to the 'real NOS' is that in the official Rolex watch certificate there is written down the name of the original first buyer. That makes the watch obviously less a virgin. It's up to you and up to the price if this meets your expectations. Me for my part I would always try to be the first and only buyer in the Rolex documents.

Super Case

Even Rolex tries to go with the flow. Reluctantly. Hesitating. So in recent years Rolex released not only the 'Sea-Dweller Deep Sea' with hulking 44 mm case and 18 mm height, they also changed their standard Oyster case to a larger one, called the 'Super Case'.

The difference is not instantly visible to the amateur eye, but it is not subtle enough to keep the elegant stance of the models.

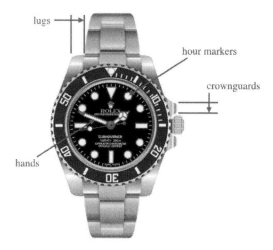

Figure 4.1: Rolex 'Super Case' and 'Maxi Dial'

The result of the newer versions with the 'Super Case' are quite different. While the 'Sea-Dweller 4000' a rather massiv sports watch with diving capabilities up to 1200 m perfectly fits the hefty new style, more subtle designs like the 'Explorer II' or the 'GMT-Master II' clearly suffer from the new looks.

Maxi Dial

Rolex dials always are about readability. The Cyclops-Lens speaks for itself. But also with the dial and hands Rolex continuously tries to do better. And so they developed the Maxi-Dial. It basically enlarges everything, especially the hour markers. In order to have more Luminova luminescent on them, their diameter was increased. Also the hands on modern Rolex models are much thicker for the same reason. And it works: readability in the dark is improved, no question.

But others say: for what price! The modern hands look almost comic-like thick and unbalanced and so does the dial. If you compare the modern Maxi-Dial models directly to the five-digit predecessors, it's obvious that a lot of elegance and delicacy is lost with the new bolder design language. And it is indeed questionable if these changes will stand the test of time.

Cyclops Lense

Ok, for some the lens on top of a lot of Rolex crystals is as big and as ugly as the eye of a cyclops. But if you try to find out the date it really helps a lot. Not only is this true for the smaller models, e.g. the 36 mm Datejust, where it is nearly obligatory, because the date ring is so small that the digits on it are simply too small to be read with the naked eye. But this also applies to the larger models with 40 mm case size, like the Sea-Dweller 4000 (which happens to not have the cyclos lens). So if you like it or not: it definitely has its value, even if you are not shortsighted.

Rattlesnake

What is more important? Usability or the impression of value? Or isn't usability the highest value as this is what every tool is about? To use it. But you must understand: perhaps this indicates the switch for Rolex being the most luxurious manufacturer of tool watches to being the most prominent manufacturer of luxury watches beyond any doubt.

What I am rambling about? The Oyster bracelet. The new Oyster bracelet has massive solid links. This was a reaction of Rolex to the brillant bracelet of the bestseller Omega Seamaster Professional from the late 1990s. Omega not only stole the 007 image from Rolex but also sold plenty of watches of surprising quality with it.

Compared to the Seamaster bracelet, the Rolex Oyster bracelet of that time felt,... (to be honest) like coming streight out of a gum machine. And with it the whole watch. And there is not very much compatibility between Rolex and gum machines at all.

Why did the old Oyster bracelets feel so... hollow? Basically because, obviously, they were. Their links were indeed hollow. And why was that? Could Rolex not afford to make proper bracelets? That is: for watches that sold for at least $3000 and usually much more?

Fact is: these hollow links did make a lot of sense and also made very proper bracelets. As they were light, very light they were very comfortable to wear. Rolex very well made them hollow on purpose.

But times change and the new bracelets aren't hollow any more, they are massive, weighty and give the whole watch a feel of heft and value. Btw: they also ballance the heftier new cases better, so they are wearing also with comfort although they are slightly heavier.

But if you shake these old hollow bracelet watches they make a silly sound. They sound a bit like a rattlesnake – rattling its tail that is of course. And that's why they are called ironically so. Rattlesnakes.

Pepsi and Coke

What have black colored sugar drinks to do with Rolex watches? Let's face it: Rolex watch names are often awkward. 'Rolex Oyster Perpetual Cosmograph', called the 'Daytona' – obviously because its written there on the dial and paticularly because it sounds much better.

But what to do with the 'Rolex Oyster Perpetual GMT-Master II' with the red/blue bezel? 'GMT Master' simply isn't sufficient since this model comes with different bezel colors (black) and color combinations (black/red, blue/red, black/blue).

So a clever guy found that blue and red are also the colors of the 'Pepsi' sugar drink brand. And ready was the nickname for the blue/red bezel version and with it for the black/red bezel alike: 'Coke'. It's valuable to note that in this one case, Pepsi could win the battle of soft drink brands as when it comes to Rolex GMT Masters, clearly the Pepsi is the original. And nothing else.

Btw: I propose for the beautiful black/black 16710 GMT Master

Figure 4.2: Rolex GMT Master II (Ref. 16710) 'Pepsi', 'Coke'

II also a fancy nick: let's call it from now on the 'Espresso'. Then there would be some continuity to the whole thing like, a drink, caffeine, black, very black color of the drink – and last but not least the reference to style itself: italian.

Pink-Lady

With Rolex watches even slight failure often is appreciated. Some of the older GMT bezels from the 1980s tended to fade over time – especially when exposed to sunlight.

And some red/blue 'Pepsi' specimen changed their color to a more light red or pink and magenta instead of blue. So to not be misunderstood: this is not a Rolex color variation for homosexuals, but simply a wear of the original color. Nevertheless this also became another holy grail of some vintage collectors.

Batman / Dark Knight

Unfortunately there wasn't another famous soft drink available with the brand colors black and blue.

So the nickname for the 'Rolex Oyster Perpetual GMT-Master II' with the blue and black bezel (Rolex code wording BLNR for

Figure 4.3: Rolex GMT Master (Ref. 1675) 'Pink Lady'

Figure 4.4: Rolex Submariner (Ref. 116710BLNR) 'Batman'

bleu-noir) had to be somewhat more creative. And while Chris Nolan's bat was flying around at the same time the BLNR came out, people found this one cool. And that's ok with me.

Stick Dial, Rectangle Dial. . .

If you are looking at the dial of a GMT with a 'stick dial' and one with a 'rectangle dial' you won't find any difference unless you know, what you are looking for.

The fact is that exactly like all the other models, also the Rolex GMT-Master II has written this name on its dial: 'GMT-Master II'. If you read special features of a GMT-Master II like 'Stick Dial' or 'Rectangle Dial' this refers to special versions of the Dial, where the roman digits 'II' are written slightly different. Yes, I am not joking. Watch enthusiasts are people who fancy perfection. And if you do that you are most likely a perfectionist yourself. And for a perfectionist nothing is small enough to not make a fuzz about.

Really a lot of fuzz is made around the different versions of the GMT Master II. The thing is, people really miss the 16710 since it was discontinued in 2008 and replaced by a rather different fellow – quite similar to the switch from the Sea-Dweller 16600 to the Sea-Dweller 'Deep Sea' 116660. Some people really liked the Deep Sea, others loathed it and wanted their old Sea-Dweller back.

And part of the fuzz in the case of the GMT is the dials that were used in the 16710 era. They basically come in at least three different types.

II ‖ II

Figure 4.5: Seriously: Rolex GMT Master II Classic, Stick, Rectangle Dial

First the normal dial. Here the 'II' in the 'GMT Master II' writing is a normal roman II with serifs (the little horizontal portions over and below the end of the vertical lines the make up the 'II'.) Yes, here we're seriously talking about the way the 'II' is written, not very much more. (please don't laugh!).

Stick Dial On the so called 'stick dial' this roman 'II' instead is written without the horizontal lines, it's sans-serif to speak in fonts terms. It was used quite seldom and it's true that the sans-serif version has a special appeal to it, it looks more modern, more distinguished – at least if you use a watchmaker's lense, because otherwise you might be having a hard time seeing the difference at all.

Rectangle Dial The 'rectangle dial' is even more scarce. Here the 'II' again has serifs (little horizontal lines above and below) but this time the vertical lines are arranged more like a rectangle, nearer to each other than in the normal dial, where the spacing between the two 'I's is larger, more old fashioned, and they nearly form a square.

This 'rectangular dial' was used towards the end of the production of the 16710. And here also is the secret to that whole dial-discussion: the 'rectangle dial' is often wrongly associated with the very rare use of the newer 3186 movement inside the 16710. But it is not true that every 'rectangle dial' GMT always has a 3186 movement, the 'rectangle dial' is not an visible sign of a model with the new movement. There are also a lot of 'rectangle dial' GMTs with the older 3185 movement. But as the 3186 movement version is very sought for, as it is very very rare, this fact started the whole 'dial-thing' with the GMT.

So what's left is that we indeed discuss here how the microscopic roman number 'II' is written on the dial. I don't think that this will be a lasting distinction between the watches. Today collectors may have the will to distinguish these hardly to be seen differences, but I think the main thing in the long run will be having a decent GMT 16710 or having it not.

Kermit

In contrast to the 'Hulk' which has a green dial as well as a green bezel, the Kermit is the anniversary Submariner from 2003 that features also a green bezel but combined with the much more decent black dial.

Figure 4.6: Rolex Submariner (Ref. 16610LV) 'Kermit'

And the green bezel ist not a ceramic bezel on a super-case as with the 'Hulk', but a more decent aluminum bezel on a classic Submariner case with a lot more decent horns.

Smurf

The starting point of the super-case Subs was the Smurf. It is called like that because it combines a blue (ceramic) bezel with a blue dial in a white-gold case.

While I consider the green-on-green combination of the 'Hulk' to green and too monsterous at a time, I really like the blue-on-blue white-gold version. It is actually a decent watch in my opinion.

Hulk

The Incredible Hulk is a comic figure conceived after the Dr. Jeckyl & Mr. Hyde myth – but here it is basically Jeckyl & Hulk. This figure is a mutated mad green giant going berserk every time he gets upset.

Figure 4.7: Rolex Submariner (Ref. 116619) 'Smurf'

Figure 4.8: Rolex Submariner (Ref. 116610LV) 'Hulk'

While in the Rolex context the 'Hulk' is the six-digit Submariner with a full green dial and a not less hulking green ceramic bezel. So basically pretty much the same as the comic character.

It originally was derived from the anniversary Submariner with a standard black dial and green bezel. And as that somehow still distinguished color combination was already taken, Rolex for the volume model went for the Hulk green/green monster alternative.

There are a lot of fans of the Hulk, but I personally am not convinced that a reasonable and decent luxury watch should be green at all. And much less a green berserking giant. But that is just like... my opinion.

4.2 Watch-ology

The watch world is full of peculiar words and ideas. Because being a watch enthusiast is a strange thing, a lot of strange ideas and terms spook around. Here are some of them for you to understand...

Exitwatch

A lot of watch enthusiasts are aware that watches, especially Rolex watches have something really addictive about them – especially owning them. As someone put it: Rolex watches are gregarious animals. They aren't alone for very long. And that is: despite their price. And despite the fact that you really cannot wear more than one at a time without totally qualifying as a jerk.

And as is often stated, this phenomen is a serious addiction and tends to endanger even stable marriages, when wifes tell their husbands the key sentence: either me or another of those watches. For some real hardcore collectors this becomes a hard decision.

So a lot of the collectors are looking for a so called 'exitwatch', a watch that satisfies them so much and calms their wish for another one so finally that they don't need another watch after this final, perfect, single, true, last, satisifying one.

Of course there is no such thing. This is self-desception, or even worse, just a simple strategy to have a good reason to buy the next watch. »Just that final one, I promise!«

Watches can be an addiction and the 'exitwatch' is a symptom.

4.3 Now, What Watch to Buy?

The first and most important thing is: watches look and feel quite differently whether you see them on a picture or on your wrist.

The thing is that watches tend to look very attraktive on those high quality product pictures but some cannot live up to that on your wrist while others that are not so shiny and bright on a picture may come to life on your wrist an fit what you want and expect quite perfectly.

So basically my advice is: wear them, that's what they are made for that's where you can find out if you really like them.

All Forms and Sizes

Let's talk about practicality. Watches today have a trend of becoming increasingly bulky and large. Where a case diameter of 36 cm was considered a watch with presence in the past, today for a men's watch 40 mm case diameter seems to be the minimum and the oversized sports watch tends to 44 mm, some even larger specimen have 46 and 48 mm cases. But diameter is not everything. The height of the case is even more important as it decides for you if your watch will fit under a cuff or not.

If you intend you wear a watch all day, don't underestimate comfort. A watch that hangs like lead on your arm will not get as much wrist time as it deserves. Only a watch that is utterly pleasant will satisfy you. And that means it should be a blessing to wear it, it should be bliss zu look at, it should have presence, you should recognize it – but first and foremost it should wear making you feel well all over. And for that it needs to wear with utter comfort.

My point of view. To be honest to you, I am a big guy. I stand over 1,90 m at more than 100 kg, athletic, and my left wrist is a little more than 20 cm in circumference. All slightly to a lot over average, depending on which country you are from. If I cannot wear a 44 mm oversized sports watch, who can.

And I can. I can wear nearly every watch on the market with comfort. Be it a 39 mm Explorer, a 40 mm Sea Dweller, a 44 mm Hublot Big Bang, a 44 mm Panerai Lunimor, all fits my wrist quite well and looks quite pleasing.

But tell you what: I prefer the smaller 40 mm sized watches. And believe it or not, even within that class there are huge differences.

E.g. at the moment a lot of people fancy the Rolex Sea-Dweller Deep Sea. And it is a great watch, no matter what. But it is too large, too heavy to wear it all day. Even it's smaller brother, the

Sea Dweller 4000 tends to do so.

Let's look at an example. Let's compare the Rolex Sea-Dweller 4000 116600 and the Rolex Yacht-Master 116622 and the Omega Seamaster Professional (Ref. 2531.80).

Both belong to the same generation of Rolex models (six-digit Reference Numbers). However the 116600 already features the so called Super-Case that tends to be larger in every proportion covering the demands of the modern market, while the 116622 still has the slightly more elegant predecessor case. Additionally the 116600 is a serious diving watch withstanding 4000 ft of water above your head while the Yacht-Master is just certified for up to 300 ft.

What determines the comfort wearing these seems to be not so much the diameter, as all of these at least on paper offer a 40 mm case (the Seamaster 41 mm). And that is quite small these days!

The watch that wears with the most comfort of these three is clearly the Yachtmaster, while the Seamaster goes second feeling much closer to the Yacht-Master than to the Sea Dweller 4000.

Even if nowadays, with a lot of 44 mm and even 48 mm watches around this might sound like a real yesterday's opinion, a large and heavy watch doesn't wear with all too much comfort. No matter what.

This is quite surprising if you compare the naked facts:

The Yacht-Master weights 139 g, and that is a lot less than the Sea Dweller 4000, that hangs with 173 g on your wrist. But in fact it is only 34 g difference and that should feel like nothing at all. To make things even more unclear: the Omega Seamaster Professional (James Bond) is with 169 g nearly as heavy as the Sea Dweller, but it wears a lot more unobtrusively.

And that is because not only the weight, but the height of the case plays also an important role. It plays a part in the weight distribution. The Sea Dweller 116600 is 15 mm in height and it really wears manly, meaning, you recognize its presence all the time, it grabs to your wrist, it holds you firm. However, the difference in wearing these both is significant. It is not dramatic, but the Sea-Dweller has a steady presence on your wrist, you feel it almost all the time on your wrist and it collides with almost every cuff and wearing a pullover you feel it under it. The Sea-Dweller ist a masculine men's watch and it demands respect from you. The Yachtmaster 116622 is 12 mm in height and that way much more similar to the Seamaster Professional with also 12 mm. You nearly do not recognize it, if you don't pay attention. If you concentrate on something else, it is as if it wasn't there at all. It's very comfortable.

In contrast the only 34 g lighter and 4 mm less thick Yacht-Master you can wear all day with almost no notice – at least not due to size and weight, you of course can look at it and admire it as often as you like. It is more laid-back, it is more elegant, in it's proportions. Despite the small difference in figures it wears totally different.

Summing up. Let's not make this too complicated. But be aware that there are differences, huge differences in these small numbers, 12 mm instead of 15 mm, 170 instead of 140 g. It sounds ridiculous, but go to a dealer and try it out. The differences are huge and they become even greater, if you don't wear a watch for just some minutes at the dealer's store, but all day from bedtime to bedtime.

So, size does matter. Even very little difference in size and weight can have a important influence on how the watch wears. Keep this in mind when you consider a Hublot Big Bang or an Audemars Piguet Royal Oak Off-Shore just because they are trendy. Keep that in mind, when you think about the Rolex Deep Sea with 44 mm in diameter, 18 mm height (that is nearly 2 cm) and a whopping 212 g. Even if you are a big guy like me. The best watch is the one you really like to wear day-in and day-out because it caress your wrist instead of clinging to it like lead.

We will not discuss other parameters like materials (of course titanium or carbon fiber cases wear much lighter), differing wrist geometries of the wearer or case geometries of the bracelet-endlinks. This would get way too much into detail. In the end it is up to the owner of the watch if he, 1) wants to wear the watch all day 2) is a collector who wears his watches depending on his mood 3) is a collector who never wears any of his watches but keeps them in his safe or even a bank vault. For the latter, these considerations might be very theoretical. But if you want to purchase the one-and-only watch for your life, wear it before you buy it.

Buy preowned, vintage or retail (new)?

A watch is something rather personal, even intimate. To be honest, I would not like to wear a watch on my skin that someone else had worn for years.

I might change my mind for a real beautiful vintage piece, like a Omega Seamaster from the 1960s or a Rolex Explorer II from the 1970s. But generally speaking, for that kind of money we are talking about, in my book everything about the watch has to be perfect – and that begins with the name on the watch id card, which is always the first owner and in the case of a pre owned watch usually not yours. That sucks.

Then I want to know how the watch was treated, e.g. if the movement might be damaged – something you cannot see if you're not a watchmaker yourself. And finally I want the watch to be and to stay perfect and that means that I do not want one little scratch on my luxury watch that cost me thousands of dollars.

There are a lot of people that recommend pre owned watches. And that might be an alternative if you'd pay a lot less for them than retail price. But if we are talking Rolex and Patek, the pre-owned prices aren't much lower than the retail prices at all, that's part of their beauty: their value is stable. Older Rolex watches, more than 20 or 30 years old, often are sold for a much higher price than they have been purchased for long ago and even much higher than a new one of the same kind would be today.

You will find examples of that on the internet. A Rolex Daytona in gold from 1973 is offered for $95.000 or a Submariner from 1965 for $13.000. That does not sound so much. But keep in mind, that the retail price back then was $500 for the Sub and $3000 for the Daytona. If you now subtract inflation, you see, why these kind of watches are considered at least value keeping investments.

That only makes sense if you dearly want exactly that watch model and you are a experienced collector – means: you know what you do and you already have all the others. Otherwise just go for the a new one.

Vintage and Vintage-Style

The Vintage Trend. What I think about new vintage style watches?

Vintage watches are en vogue today. And that is perfectly ok with me. If you value pre owned old style watches, just go ahead.

What I indeed dislike are new watches that look like old ones. In my opinion a new watch should look like a new one and (only) a vintage watch that has earned to have a patina should be allowed to look that way. New watches with patina are just ridiculous, because they pretend to be something they aren't. Style is just another word for simplicity and trueness.

This applies especially to vintage looking hour markers. Decades old luminiscent material tends to become yellow-orange-brownish. And some people really like this look. And it is absolutely ok for me, if the buy a 40 year old watch to get this worn, aged look.

But it is ridiculous if they buy a new watch with a yellow-orange-brownish colored hour markers and with a case style derived from the 1950 to *pretend* it is an old watch.

If a watch simply takes a *design* from the 1950 and is presented as a new watch, without patina, without yellow hour markers, that is ok. That is what Rolex does all the time with splendid success. They simply nearly never changed their design in all these years.

This is also important for the value of a watch over a longer period of time. The vintage look is just one more fashion style. It comes and goes.

Additionally: if you have any real luxury watch, you will never wear a fake watch any more. Perhaps on vacation or for a special occation like for a beer garden visit but usually you will sense the profound difference between the real luxury grade watch and a cheap fake.

Do I Need a Chronograph?

No, not really. But chronographs are cool. On the other hand we are talking about mechanical watches. That means that every additional function – called a complication – needs space inside the watch's case. Even if its trendy that modern watches are real big, you should be able to wear them with comfort and they should fit under the wristbands of your shirt – if you are wearing such a thing.

If you e.g. try out the Omega Speedmaster 57 with 40 mm casing and a chronograph and date complication, you will find that the watch is too big, i.e. with 16 mm simply too high on the wrist – although I am a rather tall guy at 1.90 m. The Sea-Dweller and the Panerai 112 both are 15 mm. And that is the hard limit. The Omega Seamaster Professional is only 11 mm and the Hublot Big Bang is also 16 mm but with a 44 mm diameter case and it wears vey comfortably as it is quite light.

Generally speaking Rolex makes rather small watches. That is, because the watch industry for years now tends to bigger and bigger watches and Rolex as a rather conservative brand tries not to move at all. And smaller watches are a good thing. And not to move quite far from where they are ist quite good for a stable value of the watches. Nothing destroys value more than a new model every year. Nothing keeps value more stable as continuing watch designs over decades.

What is the Most Expensive Watch?

What is the most idiotic question of the world? Our times focus on superlatives and this book surely has some. But this is not what counts. What counts is the fight against decay. What counts is reliability, stability, timelessness.

Every watchmaker can create a watch from platinum, full of diamonds like crazy and charge for that an astronomical sum that is even way beyond the material worth of the material, the stones and the craftsmanship put into all that.

Shortly Chopard released such a thing, such a monstrosity that can hardly be recognized as a watch, and prices it at $2.5 Mio. What a waste of time. That is boring, because it has nothing to do with art and simplicity and style.

Who Needs a Watch Winder?

A watch winder is a simple piece of equipment for the watch enthusiast. It consists of a electric motor and a mouting for the watch. The watch winder then will rotate the watch from time to time so that the watch is always wound up and running continuously even if you don't wear it. It is always wound when you choose to wear it. Handy, hu? So, do you need such a thing for your first Rolex?

No. And here is why: there are several reasons, why you don't need to wind your automatic watches constantly and there is only one reason or situation when you should.

Why not. Think of it. If you have an automatic watch that shows time and date and has perhaps a chronograph complication, what do you do if the watch is standing still? Simple: you unscrew the crown, pull it out, set the time and date, wind it a few times until it runs and push the crown back in and screw it again. This is so simple that it takes no more than some seconds. Then you put the watch on your wrist and it will wind up completely while you wear it moving your left hand.

If you have a manual wind watch with no automatic winding function you are completely barking up the wrong tree. The same applies to quartz watches. These are not wound by movement and you do not need a watch winder for them at all as it has no effect on them.

So for what purpose would I need such a thing at all? For a special type of watches: there are watches that do not only show you the time and date, but also the weekday (e.g. The Rolex Daydate). Some even have a precise calender function the will show you the correct day, moonphase and date for the next 100 years, every day. This basically means that you will never have to correct the date on the first of march, not even in a leap year – at least not for the next 100 years.

But this of course only works if the watch never stops running. If it stops it is quite complicated to set it to the right time, date, month and year again just using the crown. It might turn out to be horribly complicated. Surely this is something you won't want to do every time you did not wear your watch for one week.

For these watches a watch winder is not just handy but next to a must.

But isn't it also handy to have all my conventional automatic watches (even without complex calender functions) are all wound and I only have to take them to wear them without ever winding them? Yes, sure it is.

But also keep in mind the the watches are mechanical. An mechanical always and at the same time means *wear*. However minimal that wear is due to high tech bearings, a watch that runs 24/7 will show more wear than a watch that runs now and then. So if you have several watches you rotate through on your wrist, winding them from time to time and keeping them still the rest of the time will simply minimize wear in the movement.

4.4 'Luxury' Replica Watches

Ok, when we talk about luxury watches, we need to have a look on the down side of this market: let's talk about replica watches for a moment. And first of all: a fake watch, even if it is called a 'replica' is not a luxury watch, even if it more or less looks exactly like one or even is nearly as expensive as the original, in truth a fake watch it is the exact opposite of a luxury watch: it is utterly worthless.

On the internet there is even a whole war going on between the fake sellers promoting their product, telling people in their typical east-asian style how nice the watches are and how easy it is to get one and on the other side the representatives of the watchmaking industry fighting against them by threatening potential buyers with jail, because they basically import illegal goods into their country. However, as usual the threatening party doesn't have the sympathy on their side.

And don't let them fool you. Both are far from being objective. And the whole thing is going on, because fake luxury watches is a multi-million dollar market.

So Close and Yet so Far

Wearing a fake Rolex is a bit like wearing a Batman mask for a party. You are not Batman, but it is some fun if you don't take it too seriously. At least for some time. It surely wears of quickly, and as the Batman mask you won't wear it all day.

For Rolex however it is a crime, as there is not only a guy who wears their trademarks but more important the most precious thing a luxury watch maker has is in danger: scarcity. If everyone has a (fake) Rolex they are not seldom and precious any more but daily business. And everyone who wants to separate himself from the crowd by wearing a really expensive and unique watch will switch to another manufacturer. That way the wearer of the fake watch basically steals from Rolex because he damages their standing as a maker of real scarce and outstandingly precious goods.

But this problem also exists if you wear a watch that looks quite similar to a Rolex, but isn't like e.g. the Rolex inhouse budget line 'Tudor'. These are watches that look very similar like the Rolex original but feature 'only' a ETA movement and are not so shiny and high end like the Rolex branded ones. And there are hundreds of watchmakers that have a watch in their collection that looks more or less like the all-classic Rolex Submariner. These all if you look at it from that perspective take away exclusivity from Rolex.

So if you can live with that, you may read on. Then the question, whether you are allowed to be interested in a fake luxury watch completely depends on what you expect from it.

However the thing you need to understand most of all is: a fake watch is a watch without value. You cannot resell it, because it is a illegal product. Once you give your money away for it, this money is gone forever.

So a fake luxury watch is in truth exactly the opposite of a real luxury watch, which, as we found out, is supposed to keep or even increase its value over the many decades of its existence. If you don't like a real luxury watch any more, you can sell it, often for more than 50% of the price you payed, even if you had it for 20 or more years. If it is a Rolex Daytona, you may expect to sell it for a far higher price than you purchased it for. Even if you take inflation into account. A fake you can only throw into the trashcan.

However there might be one or the other use for even such a product.

Increasingly Criminal Flavours

Fake watches come in different price ranges mostly depending on their movement. We are ignoring those fakes you can buy on a beach from a guy who walks up and down the waterline or those you can buy at street markets in the south. These usually are total crab, made from extremely cheap materials and often resemble the original only if you suffer from utter blindness.

The better ones that really look similar to the original, even on the second closer look, come in three flavours:

There are the relatively cheap models with a cheap quartz movement for around $150. Then there are mid range watches with an asian mechanical movement for around $500 and finally there are quite expensive fakes with an exact asian copy of a swiss ETA movement that are offered for over $1000 and they are marketed by saying they had a 'swiss' movement, something that is obviously not the case.

I consider these watches increasingly criminal with their price. And here is why:

It is one thing buying a fake watch with a quartz movement for $150, while the original costs $10,000. The buyer obviously does not want a real Rolex, but a fun watch with a fancy, classic and stylish design that looks like a Rolex but obviously isn't. Neither the price tag nor the intention of the potential buyer is nowhere near pretending something untrue. Perhaps it is even some kind of marketing for Rolex, as the fake buyer perhaps likes his watch so much, that he someday wants to have the real one.

Noone who would buy a real Rolex would instead buy a quartz fake. The two markets simply don't intersect and so both kinds of watches aren't competitors at all.

In my opinion the whole discussion around these cheap fakes works a litte bit like the complaints of the music industry on illegal downloads. The music industry calculated it like this: ok, there are 1000 illegal downloads of our CD and that means, our losses due to illegal downloads are the equivalent of having sold these 1000 CDs. And that was of course completely and even willingly wrong, because perhaps in reality a maximum of 25% of these 1000 downloaders would have bought this CD if it hadn't been available for free – perhaps even less.

And this is even more true with these cheap Rolex fakes. Just because the market of luxury watches over $5000 is much smaller and the price gap between the fakes for $150 and the true $5000 or more for the real one is much broader. These 1000 people who bought the fake do in no way mean that Rolex could have sold 1000 real Rolex watches to these exact 1000 buyers. Here I would estimate it being perhaps 1or 2 of these 1000 people that would be able and willing to buy a real one, if there was no fake available. They'd just buy a Seiko, a Citizen or a Casio or whatever other fashion brand. These are the companies that in truth suffer from the losses of the fake manufacturers directly.

Ok, still the fake watchmakers use trademarked names and symbols, which they shouldn't, but the financial loss Rolex has due to these kind of fakes should be near zero.

In my opinion the situation is different with those quite expensive fakes with even mechanical movements. They sometimes even play in the same price range as the originals and try to apply to the same customers. E.g. a real Omega Speedmaster might be around $2000 while the ETA-fake version is $1000. That is really a problem for Omega.

Apart from the fact that everyone who buys the fake instead of the original to save that 50% must be a total idiot as he buys something worthless for his 50%-off pricetag, in my book this is highly criminal, because these fakes indeed are a real hazard to the market of the originals. This is product piracy of the worst kind. If someone sells a fake for being the real one, it's even worse.

Perfect Imitations?

Are fake luxury watches so perfect imitations that even a watch-maker could not identify the fake?

There is the rumor, but in my opinion, no. Yes, the well made fakes look really good, they look quite similar to the original and they can even be some fun.

But the truth is, you cannot imitate perfection with anything else but perfection. That means: as the original swiss made luxury watches aim at perfection in every possible way, you cannot copy them without the same struggle for perfection. And you cannot do this, not even in China, for $150. So there are always shortcomings about those fake watches you will be easily able to spot if you got some experience in the look and perfection of the originals.

If you ever had a real Rolex on your wrist and had a closer look at it, you even can see and feel the differences to original but lesser luxury watches like e.g. an Omega. Just wind it and you feel the perfection of the Rolex movement. The Rolex casing is the next point. It is so perfect, every shape, every surface, every detail is without the slightest flaw, everything is in perfect symmetry, every material used is treated to look utterly beautiful. It takes you no more than a few seconds to see and feel, that a real Rolex is a completely different beast than even an original Tag-Heuer or a Breitling.

A fake one misses this attention to detail more or less completely. You will see that immediately. The materials are bad, the finish is cheap, the precision of the dial is absent. If you only have the fake in your hands, it might look quite good. If you compare fake to original or if you once had an original in your hands, you immediately see the differences. Then the fake just looks like garbage. And every watchmaker of course can see these differences with ease.

Could it be Legitimate to Buy a Fake?

Buying a fake watch is never legal. But in my opinion it might be legitimate if you cause no damage to anyone but yourself. So the only fake watch I would accept anyone to buy is a cheap quartz watch, that is no competition to the real one at all, and only if for a special purpose like e.g.:

1. Perhaps you want a watch with a great design to wear it on the beach, on vacation or in any other rugged watch-unfriendly environment. Perhaps you even own the original one, but do not want it to catch scratches in some situation, why shouldn't you grab a fake one for riding the bike or going climbing if you want to be on the save side and having the original keeping its perfect condition and its value? (Well, obviously because you won't fancy the fake at all if you know the original.) In my book this would be an legitimate idea.

2. Perhaps you consider buying the original but want a kind of testing phase, a preview for some weeks what it might be like wearing such a watch on a daily basis, before you spent 10 or 20 grand and later don't like it so much. Especially with the trend for watches with large diameters of 44 mm and more at heights of 15 mm and more it might take some time to find out, if such a watch fits your wrist or perhaps not. In such a case a cheap but well done fake could be of some (testing-) value for you.

3. Perhaps you even might want to mislead a thief who wants to steal your real watch by presenting a fake dummy to him instead. You perhaps choose to do this for a vacation or even at home.

4. You might even really like the design of a watch but will never be able to purchase the original, because it is $50,000 or $250,000. If you really love the look of a watch but at the same time do not intend to look like someone you are not, this would be ok for me. It's like purchasing one of those Ferrari replicas you can put on a Camaro basis. It's far from the same thing but some fun for a while. And it is a kind of homage at the same time and shows your appreciation.

The important question here is: do you buy the fake for yourself or to impress others. It's ok, if you do it for yourself and your private fun. After all, even a fake luxury watch is still a watch, you can use to find out what time it is.

But you should never purchase a fake watch pretending it being the real thing – not to yourself and of course not to others. And that's what the fakes with mechanical movement do. This would be being untrue to yourself and to others and even stealing from the real watchmakers. It is not good for you and your self-esteem as you will become a fake yourself over time.

Finally, you always feel the difference wearing a real luxury watch or wearing just a fake.

Recommendations

We of course would also recommend to you the following ebooks...

- Rolex Watches

- Collecting Luxury Watches

- Ten Fun Things to do with Luxury Watches

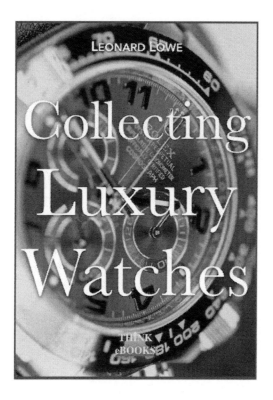

Collecting Luxury Watches

5/5 Stars ***** Great book for watch enthusiasts! This is the second e-book from this author, that I've read. He has a nice, clear writing style and definitely he has lots of insight on what makes a particular watch brand and watch model valuable. I thought the omission of Grand Seiko was somewhat odd, but it is still a great book.« (July 18, 2017)

Leonard Lowe wrote three books about luxury watches: Luxury Watches, Rolex Watches and Ten Fun Things to do with Luxury Watches. And here is his fourth one, his most personal one, with the most insight in his own personal collection and his thoughts why and when he purchased his collectibles. A personal history of becoming a watch enthusiast despite starting out an ordinary person with a lot of hints and thoughts on purchasing and collecting luxury watches.

»I never decided to be a watch collector. It just happened somehow. This book finally tells the story of my passion for luxury watches, how I learned about them, what I considered before and after purchasing my pieces and how it is owning and wearing them. I am sure a lot of my considerations will help the new and even the advanced watch lover to learn even more about watches, about collecting them or – if you're not a collector – just about finding the right one-and-only watch for your wrist. What you will find in this ebook is an amusing, entertaining and insightful story of my personal experiences with luxury watches. Have fun...!«

Join Leonard Lowe on his journey through the world of luxury watches and find a lot of useful and inspiring insights about this compelling hobby.

Links to (purchase) this book are here:
    http://www.think-ebooks.com/collecting-luxury-watches/

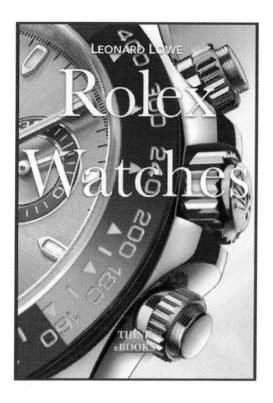

Rolex Watches

5/5 Stars ***** Well worth reading and at a fair price: »This is a very useful and clearly written primer for anyone who is interested in Rolex watches. All of the modern and many of the vintage watches are covered. The compact format is a handy feature.« (Harrell, March 4. 2017)

5/5 Stars ***** MUY BUENO.« (Juan Carlos Camino, March 15. 2017)

This ebook provides a lot of purchase relevant background information on the most important Rolex models. With this ebook you will be able to select the watch you want to purchase with ease. You will have a quick overview of the Rolex models and understand why they are there and why some models are considered more important and valuable than others.

The Rolex lineup of watches evolved over time. And like every naturally evolving structure it is a bit confusing at the first and often also second look. It helps a lot to understand when and why which model was introduced and what changes it got over time. You also will be able to understand the Rolex vintage collectors' movement, that values old Rolex models much higher than the modern lineup.

This ebook tries to sort this out a bit. To understand what watch is meant for what audience, what differences are there between the models, and how the whole thing did evolve since the 1950s, this book will give you some important advice.

It is no question if you will find the best watch for you within the Rolex world, if you just know the details we present to you in this ebook. And selecting the right Rolex is always a matter of money. So be wise and learn, before you buy.

This is not a Rolex sales catalogue. In contrary to such an approach we tried to cover all the information that is not given on official websites but nevertheless should make it much clearer, how the Rolex models are connected to each other and what might be the right one for your wrist.

Links to (purchase) this book are here:
    http://www.think-ebooks.com/rolex-watches/

Ten fun Things to do with Luxury Watches

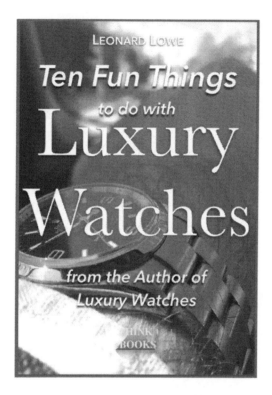

A book not only about collecting watches...

Ten fun things you can do with luxury watches... well, ok, it ended up being thirteen things, not ten. But that already says a lot. And no, it not only says that you get 30% more than you payed for... it says something about watches, about having watches as a hobby and about the fun you can have with them. Because basically it is always fun to deal with something beautiful, with something perfectionistic and with some piece of art. It means dealing with something higher than you are and that alone lifts you up.

A luxury watch is not just a watch. You can do a lot of smart, fun and interesting things with a watch, inspired by a watch or in companianship with a watch.

This ebook will give you some ideas, inspiration and even reason, why some people are interested in these very special watches and often frantically collect them. Keep in mind: we are talking about watches that are 'defined' by these peculiar characteristics: they are made in Switzerland and they are at least $5000.

Of course there is more to a 'real' luxury watch than these two base characteristics. A lot of people narrow the whole industry that consists of dozens of companies down to about 9 really important companies: Rolex, Omega, Breitling (that much about the companies you probably already heard about) and there is Patek-Philippe, Audemars Piguet and Vacheron Constantain, who are called the Holy Trinity (!) and there is Jaeger-LeCoultre, Breguet and IWC, who are... well... also very important. For a first take you can ignore all the others. Perhaps you will encounter Hublot and Panerai and other brands that try to distinguish themselves from the mainstream. They can be entertaining too...

Watches are a really rewarding hobby. You can do a lot of things with watches and around them. They are a kind of technology that is around for about 300 years and the oldest companies in the market are nearly there from the very beginning. So you can learn a lot about very different areas on this very peculiar, very special and very secluded market: about luxury of course, also about style, about beauty, about technology, about marketing, about riches and rich people, about capital, money and lasting value, about time and timelessness, about fun and application, about diving, space travel, precision measurement and last but not least about the biggest secret of them all: about time.

So let's have a little stroll around and look what watches have got in for you. There is something that you will find interesting or even inspiring. Trust me and come with me for a few precious moments together...

Please find links to this book at all the major ebook stores as well as the paperback edition at

http://think-ebooks.com/ten-fun-things-to-do-with-luxury-watches/

Tell us Your Opinion

Thank you very much for reading this ebook. We would of course very much appreciate if you liked the ebook. If you have any further questions on the subject, have some criticism or ideas for improvement please feel free to tell us your thoughts: please write to leo.lowe@rocketmail.com or visit our website at THINK-ebooks.com http://think-ebooks.com

Printed in Great Britain
by Amazon